100 BATTLES

THAT SHAPED WORLD HISTORY

Samuel Willard Crompton

A Bluewood Book

This edition produced and published in 1997 by Bluewood Books
A Division of The Siyeh Group, Inc.,
P.O. Box 689
San Mateo, CA 94401

ISBN 0-912517-27-1

Printed in USA
10, 9, 8, 7, 6, 5, 4, 3, 2, 1

Designed by Eric Irving
Copy Edited by Linnea Due
Edited by Barbara Krystal
Cover illustration by Tony Chikes

About the Author:
Samuel Willard Crompton teaches American and European history at Holyoke Community College in Massachusetts. Keenly interested in American biography, he has served as a Writing Fellow for the *American National Biography* (Oxford University Press, 1998) and contributed many sections to the *Cambridge Dictionary of American Biography* (Cambridge University Press, 1995). He holds degrees from Framingham State College and Duke University. A free-lance writer for over ten years, he is the author of *100 Wars that Shaped World History* (Bluewood Books, 1997) and *Presidents of the United States* (Smithmark, 1992). An avid bicyclist and traveler, he has seen much of North America by plane, train, car, and foot. Long interested in public service, he has been a tax preparer and telephone operator. He lives in western Massachusetts, a rural region that has produced many remarkable Americans, including Cecil B. DeMille and Russell H. Conwell, and has served as poetic inspiration for many others, including Archibald MacLeish and Richard Wilbur.

Picture Acknowledgements:
Bluewood Books Archives: all pages except;
U.S. Library of Congress: 79, 80, 83, 84, 86t, 87, 89, 101, 104, 106
U.S. National Archives: 62, 63, 64, 65, 67, 72, 74, 76, 82, 85, 86b, 88, 90, 91, 92, 93, 94, 95, 96, 98, 99, 100, 102, 103, 105
National Portrait Gallery: 51
U.S. Military Institute: 97, 107

TABLE OF CONTENTS

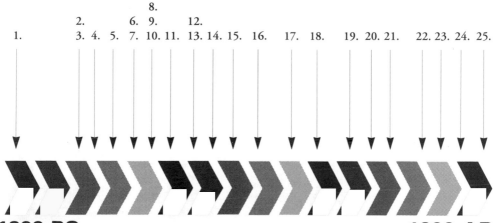

1300 BC

1200 AD

37.   44.   49.
26. 27. 28. 29. 30.   31. 32. 33.   34. 35. 36. 38. 39. 40. 41. 42. 43. 45. 46. 47. 48. 50.

1200 AD   4   **1750 AD**

53. BATTLE OF QUEBEC CITY   *60*
September 13, 1759

54. BATTLE OF QUIBERON BAY   *61*
November 14, 1759

55. BATTLES OF LEXINGTON
AND CONCORD   *62*
April 19, 1775

56. BATTLE OF BUNKER HILL   *63*
June 17, 1775

57. BATTLE OF TRENTON   *64*
December 26, 1776

58. BATTLES OF SARATOGA   *65*
September 19 - October 17, 1777

59. BATTLE AND SIEGE OF GIBRALTAR   *66*
June 24, 1779 - February 7, 1783

60. BATTLE AND SIEGE OF YORKTOWN   *67*
September 28 - October 19, 1781

61. BATTLE OF VALMY   *68*
September 20, 1792

62. BATTLE OF THE NILE   *69*
August 1, 1798

63. BATTLE OF TRAFALGAR   *70*
October 21, 1805

64. BATTLE OF AUSTERLITZ   *71*
December 2, 1805

65. BATTLE OF NEW ORLEANS   *72*
January 8, 1815

66. BATTLE OF WATERLOO   *73*
June 18, 1815

67. BATTLES OF JUNIN AND AYACUCHO   *74*
August 4 and December 9, 1824

68. BATTLES OF THE ALAMO
AND SAN JACINTO   *75*
February 23 - March 6, and April 21, 1836

69. BATTLE OF CHAPULTEPEC   *76*
September 13, 1847

70. BATTLE OF ANTIETAM   *77*
September 17, 1862

71. BATTLE OF GETTYSBURG   *78*
July 1-3, 1863

72. BATTLE OF SEDAN   *79*
September 1, 1870

73. BATTLE OF THE LITTLE BIG HORN   *80*
June 25, 1876

74. BATTLE OF ADOWA   *81*
March 1, 1896

75. BATTLE OF SAN JUAN HILL   *82*
(ACTUALLY KETTLE HILL)
July 1, 1898

76. BATTLE AND SIEGE
OF PORT ARTHUR   *83*
June 1, 1904 - January 2, 1905

77. BATTLE OF TSUSHIMA STRAITS   *84*
May 27, 1905

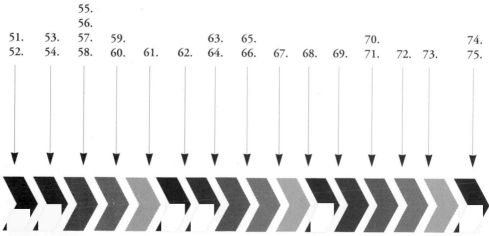

1750 AD

1900 AD

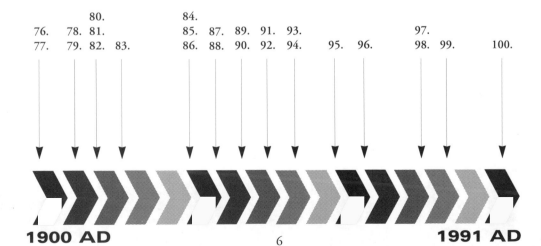

1900 AD

1991 AD

INTRODUCTION

From the first recorded battles in the Middle East to the battle for **Kuwait** in the **Gulf War**, men (and sometimes women) have taken up arms for personal, political, and economic goals. Religion, territory, glory and the pursuit of wealth have all played roles in motivating humans toward battle. At base is a desire to best one another that is often met in combat, whether it be through swordplay or the exchange of missiles.

Battles claim an everlasting hold upon memory and the human psyche. Throughout human history, chroniclers and historians have sought to preserve the record of the great battles, so that later generations would know of the leaders, contestants, armies and outcomes that created the borders and introduced cultural influences in nations today.

Which were the truly great battles of history? This is of course debatable, and numerous historians have tried to answer the question. A particularly notable effort was made by Major General J.F.C. Fuller in *A Military History of the Western World* (1954). But even experts disagree on what were the most important or most crucial battles. One of the best answers given to this sort of speculation was made by the **Marquis de Lafayette**, a Frenchman who came to the United States in 1777 to fight with the Americans as they won their independence from Great Britain. Later, in his middle age, Lafayette met Emperor **Napoleon Bonaparte**. Napoleon scoffed at the small size of the armies that had fought in the American Revolution. After all, only 20,000 men were present on both sides at **Saratoga** and only 25,000 were present at **Yorktown**. By contrast, Napoleon would lead 600,000 men against Russia in the year 1812. Lafayette

responded, "It was the grandest of causes fought with the smallest of means."

Such is the approach of this book, to determine to what extent the battle shaped the outcome of a war or conflict, and to what extent that conflict shaped world history. Some battles have been selected that were indeed awe-inspiring in their size, such as **Arabela** in 331 BC, while others such as the **Metaurus** in 207 BC were notable for their small size. The common denominator is that each of the battles selected had a major impact upon warfare and human history.

Marked changes in strategy and weaponry have transformed the face of battles over the centuries. Middle Eastern combat in the time of the Egyptians centered on the chariot, which later gave way to the cavalry group. Greek and Roman infantryman dominated the Mediterranean world for centuries with their **phalanx** and legion formations, but these solid infantry groups were later swept aside during the era of Central Asian horsemen: the Huns, Mongols, and Turks. Fortifications made during the Middle Ages stood for centuries but then crumbled with the advent of gunpowder and artillery in the fifteenth century. More recently, the musket gave way to the rifle, which yielded to the machine gun; the ship of the line was replaced by the battleship and then the aircraft carrier.

Armies still depend upon individual soldiers, and warfare is still intended to advance the goals of a nation or tribe. What seems most likely is that battles will continue to evolve and that developments in strategy and weaponry will emerge to surprise soldiers, generals, historians and civilians alike.

1. KADESH
1294 BC

Around the turn of the fourteenth century BC, a new kingdom arose in **Asia Minor** (what is today called Turkey) to challenge the power of **Egypt** in the Middle East. The **Hittite** kingdom remains relatively unknown to historians today, but what is clear is that its people used iron weapons at a time when the Egyptians and almost everyone else were still using bronze to make weapons. When the Hittites began to contest with Egypt for control of the territory of present-day Israel and Lebanon, the Egyptians decided to strike a deadly blow against the new kingdom. Egyptian Pharaoh **Ramses II** (RAM seez) recruited an army of 20,000 men, including infantry and charioteers. He was opposed by a Hittite army of 8,500 infantry and 10,500 charioteers (the Hittites brought 3,500 chariots to the battle).

The battle was fought southeast of **Kadesh** on the **Orontes River** in Syria. At first, the Hittites seemed to have the advantage. The weight of their initial chariot assault threw the Egyptians into confusion, and the Hittites penetrated to the main camp of the Egyptian army. Many of the Hittite soldiers spent their time plundering the camp, which allowed the Egyptians time to rally. The battle ended in a bloody, inconclusive draw. Ramses II recorded the battle in great detail on monuments and obelisks, but his recordings did not take notice of the fact that Kadesh left matters much as they had been before: a powerful Hittite kingdom to the north and the venerable Egyptian empire to the south, with a no-man's land in between. Kadesh shaped world history because it left that no-man's land intact. This area (present-day Lebanon, Syria, Israel and Jordan) later developed a number of small kingdoms (as opposed to mighty empires). Those small kingdoms produced important discoveries for the future of the world. For example, the kingdom of **Phoenicia** in present-day Lebanon developed the world's first phonetic alphabet (21 letters) and the kingdoms of **Judea** and **Israel** developed monotheistic religious practice.

Hittite Warriors

By 500 BC, the **Persian Empire** had replaced the **Babylonian** and **Assyrian** empires that had existed in the areas of present-day Iran and Iraq. The Persians were the best fighters of their day; relentless horsemen who had defeated their rivals time and again. In 490 BC, the Persian King **Darius I** (duh RY uhs) **(556-486 BC)** sent an army of 20,000 men by sea against the small peninsula of Greece. The Greeks lived in small **city-states** that were independent of one another; the world's first experiment in democracy was being conducted in the city state of **Athens.** To the Persians, their incursion against Greece was intended merely to enforce Persian rule in yet another region, but to the Greeks, repelling the invaders seemed crucial for the survival of democracy.

Darius' men landed on a narrow beach 20 miles north of Athens. They settled in to await a possible attack by the Athenians and Plataeans (11,000 strong) who stood on a hillside overlooking the beach. At this critical moment, most neutral observers would have favored the Persians, a people who had been fighting and conquering for nearly 100 years. It was the Greeks who moved first that day. Led by **Miltiades** (mihl-TY-uh- deez) **(died 488 BC)** and **Callimachus**, the Greeks advanced down the slope in a running charge against the Persians. As they made their way through the barrage of arrows released by the Persian archers, the Greeks sought to engage in hand-to-hand combat. The Persian center held, but both of the Persian flanks gave way under the Greek assault. Within one hour's time, the Persians were

thoroughly defeated, with 6,400 left dead while the rest escaped to their ships and returned to **Asia Minor** (Turkey). The Greeks lost 192 men. When modern historians attempt to account for the overwhelming Greek victory, they make much of the fact that the Greeks fought in a straight-ahead formation while the Persians were accustomed to skirmishing, or fighting on the flanks.

Marathon was one of the truly decisive battles of all time. The Greek victory on the beach enabled Athens and Greece to maintain their freedom from Persia and to continue to build the framework of a democracy that would be handed down to Europe and eventually the New World. Also, the concept and tradition of the 26-mile run known as a "Marathon" came from the Greek runner **Pheidippedes** (fi-dip-I-deez), who ran to Athens with news of the Greek victory and then died of exhaustion.

The Battle of Marathon

SALAMIS
September 20, 480 BC

Xerxes (Zhurk-sees) **(519-465 BC)**, known as the **King of Kings**, succeeded his father **Darius I (556-486 BC)** as Emperor of Persia. Furious with the defeat at **Marathon** (see no. 2), Xerxes planned a grand invasion that would swallow up Athens and all of Greece. He led a large Persian army (some historians estimate a force of 300,000 men) through Turkey, across the Hellespont, and into Greece by way of **Thrace** and **Macedonia**. His men were supplied by a fleet that brought food to the meat-eating Persians (the Greeks were vegetarians).

Xerxes and his men were temporarily halted at **Thermopalayae** (thuhr MAHP ul lee), a narrow mountain pass to the north of Athens. There, some 300 Spartan warriors fought a long battle of attrition and managed to delay the Persian advance and to invoke a large number of casualties to the invaders. When the Persians finally broke through and killed the defenders at Thermopalayae, it looked as if the Greeks had been defeated.

Xerxes soon occupied Athens and appeared ready to conquer the rest of Greece.

The Greeks, however, had a new weapon; the **trireme** ship that had been developed in the ten years since the battle of Marathon. When Xerxes entered Athens, he found a deserted city, since the Athenian fleet managed to evacuate most of the people and bring them to the island of **Salamis**, to the south. The stage was set for a naval battle that would either confirm the Persian conquest of Greece or throw the whole matter open to question once again.

Xerxes had a throne placed on a hill overlooking the bay where the battle was fought. His fleet of over 1,000 Persian **galleys** entered the bay and confronted the Greek fleet of 370 trireme vessels. The battle was fought all day long. The Greeks persevered and won the battle due to two factors: first, the Greeks used fire as a weapon, setting Persian ships aflame. Second, because the Greeks knew the waters better, they were able to outmaneuver their opponents in the close ship-to-ship fighting. At the end of the day, Xerxes saw a wrecked and defeated Persian fleet limp away .

Lacking the supply line that his fleet had provided, Xerxes withdrew from Athens and Greece. He went back to **Asia Minor**, though he left behind a substantial Persian force that was completely defeated the following spring by the Greeks. The combination of Marathon and Salamis ended any chance of a Persian takeover of Greece.

The Battle of Salamis

After ending the threat of Persian invasion (see no. 2 and no. 3), the Greek city-states began to fight against one another. The greatest rivalry was between **Athens**, traditionally a sea power and trading city, and **Sparta**, which relied upon its indomitable warriors. The envy and distrust between these two powers led to the famous **Peloponnesian War** (Pehl uh puh NEE shuhn), which lasted from 432 to 403 BC. At first Athens was led by the brilliant politician **Pericles (495-429 BC)**, who urged his countrymen to avoid fighting the Spartans on land. Instead, the Athenians remained within the walls that encircled Athens and struck against the Spartans and their allies by sea.

Pericles died while the war was still in its early stages, and his successors chose to wage a more aggressive war. They wasted men and material in a futile siege of Syracuse, Sicily, and by 410 BC, Athens was running low on men, morale and money.

The Spartans sought aid in the form of money from an old enemy of all the Greeks: Persia. Reinforced by Persian gold, the Spartans and their allies built a fleet to rival that of Athens and appointed **Lysander** (li-san-der) (**died 395 BC**), as their first admiral. Knowing that Athens depended upon food supplies brought in by its ships, the Spartans sought to fight the Athenian fleet as it brought grain from the Black Sea to Athens, meeting the Athenians at **Aegospotami**, in the Hellespont.

As some historians have commented, the entire Peloponnesian War resembled an elephant fighting a whale. Now, the elephant had developed fins and was challenging the whale in its own element. Lysander struck the surprised Athenians, and the battle, such as it was, turned into a complete rout, with 173 Athenian ships captured after their crews beached them. The 3,000 to 4,000 men who

Pericles

were taken prisoner were all killed, due to the long-standing hatred between Athens and Sparta. This defeat sealed the fate of Athens. Within a year's time, a peace was concluded. The walls that had surrounded Athens for over a century were pulled down, and Athens had to yield possession of the empire she had built within the Aegean Sea. The Peloponnesian War was over; Sparta had won, and yet all of Greece had lost. The golden age of Pericles would not return.

5. LEUCTRA
July 371 BC

Sparta's dominance of the Greek peninsula was as noxious to the Greek city-states as Athenian dominance had been. Within a generation of the **Battle of Aegospotami** (see no. 4), Greeks were beginning to seek a further degree of freedom from Sparta. One of the leaders of the new movement was **Epaminondas** (e-pam-I-non-das) **(418?-362 BC)**, son of the king of **Thebes** (theebz), another Greek city-state. As a boy, Epaminondas was forced to spend time in Sparta as a hostage, to guarantee the good behavior of his father. A keen observer of both human nature and military tactics, he watched the Spartans closely and came to understand why they had become known as the best warriors of their day.

When he became king of Thebes in his own right, Epaminondas refused to pay tribute to Sparta. He then faced a Spartan invasion of his territory, something that every Greek leader feared greatly. The Theban army was drawn up ten miles west of Thebes, in present-day Voiotia, Greece. The Spartans had 11,000 men; the Thebans had roughly 6,000 soldiers. Not only were the odds against them, but the Thebans knew-as all Greeks knew, that the Spartan warriors had been unconquerable since the **Battle of Thermopalayae**, 110 years earlier. However, Epaminondas had his own ideas on Sparta's invincibility.

The Spartans deployed their men in their traditional manner, placing the best warriors on their right flank. Epaminondas did the reverse, placing his best men on his left flank, directly opposite the Spartan best. He also arranged his right flank in an **echelon** that pointed away from the Spartans, thus declining to fight in the usual straight ahead clash. The Theban left, which was arranged in a column 80 feet wide and 150 foot deep, quickly broke through the Spartan right flank. The Spartans fought stubbornly and bravely, but made no tactical innovations to respond to this attack. Within a few hours, Epaminondas had overcome the Spartans who lost 2,000 men, including **Cleombrotus**, the king of Sparta. The Theban loss is unrecorded, but believed to have been light. By the end of the day Thebes had emerged as the new military power in Greece. The battle also confirmed that coordinated troop movements could overcome even the most rigorously stalwart fighting men.

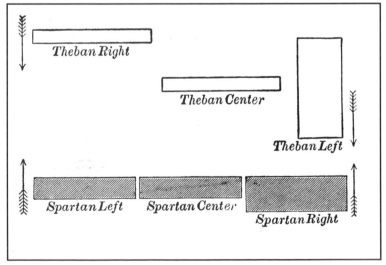

Battle plan for Leuctra

6. ISSUS
October 333 BC

Philip of Macedon conquered **Thebes** and became the undisputed master of Greece in 338 BC. The hard-riding and hard-drinking Macedonian soldiers intended to march against Persia next, but Philip died prematurely. He was succeeded by his son **Alexander (356-323 BC)**, later known as **Alexander the Great**, who had led the cavalry charge that had defeated the Thebans. Seldom in history has such a great military leader as Philip been succeeded by a son who turned out to be even more of a military genius than his father.

The Battle of Issus

Alexander led 30,000 Macedonian troops across the Hellespont into **Asia Minor** in 333 BC. He defeated a Persian army of the same size at the Granicus River and marched eastward. In southeastern Asia Minor, he was met and challenged by a Persian army of 90,000 men, led by King **Darius III (380?-330 BC)**, who, like his predecessor **Xerxes**, was known as the **King of Kings**. Darius lay his army along Alexander's lines of supplies and forced the Macedonians into battle at **Issus**, on the Payas River, near Iskenderun in present-day Turkey.

The battle was fought on a narrow plain between the mountains and the sea, which prevented Darius from using the whole of his army (some chroniclers speculate he had as many as 500,000 men). In addition, Darius' force was made up of soldiers from many different cultural and national groups (Bactrians, Persians, Phoenicians, even Greek mercenaries), while Alexander's men were a cohesive core of troops that knew only victory.

Darius began by advancing cavalry on his flanks, hoping to draw the Macedonians to where his greater numbers could attack them. The Macedonian cavalry routed the Persian horsemen and then went over to the offense, driving against the main body of the Persian army. There appeared to be no reason the Persians could not prevail, but the multinational composition of his army worked against Darius. His men did not coordinate well with one another, and the sudden advance of the Macedonian **phalanx** (feylangks), a wall of swords and spears, developed by Philip and perfected by Alexander, terrified them. Only Darius' Greek mercenaries fought on; the other parts of the Persian army disintegrated in the face of Alexander's attack. Darius fled from the scene of the battle. He and his men were pursued by the Greek cavalry but they managed to escape. The same could not be said of some 15,000 men of the Persian army who were killed, nor of Darius' queen and family, who were captured by the Greeks in the aftermath of the battle. One day's fighting had gained for Alexander undisputed control of Asia Minor and the areas of present-day Lebanon and Syria as well.

Following his great victory at **Issus** (see no. 6), **Alexander the Great (356-323 BC)** captured the Phoenician city of **Tyre** and proceeded through Egypt before he turned again to face the Persians. Alexander had already captured one-third of the Persian Empire, and King **Darius III (380?-330 BC)** sent envoys asking Alexander for terms of peace. Alexander scorned the offers. To him, victory was either all-encompassing or nothing; there could be no middle ground. After spending time in Egypt, where he was told by Egyptian priests that he was the son of **Amun**, the sun god, Alexander led his men back into Asia to confront the Persians again.

For this battle, Darius assembled an even greater army to meet the Macedonians. At least 250,000 soldiers (multinational rather than all Persian) assembled on the plain of **Arbela**, sometimes called **Guagamela**, near present-day Mosul in northern **Iraq**. Darius spent days preparing the battleground. He had his men sweep the plain clean of brush and debris, so that his chariots and horsemen could be deployed to their greatest advantage. He had 200 chariots, 15 elephants, as many as 40,000 horsemen, and 200,000 infantry, gathered together from all parts of the vast Persian empire. The size and strength of his army underscored how rattled Darius was. A larger army could not have given him true confidence, for he believed that Alexander was virtually unbeatable. Alexander thought the same; as did an increasing number of Alexander's men who had marched from one victory to another for over two years.

Alexander drew up his 40,000-man army lurching toward the left flank of the Persian army. As the battle began, the Greeks continued to move toward their right, forcing Darius to move his men to assist against the concentrated attack. Darius released his charioteers and elephants, and both were repulsed by Macedonians using arrows and javelins.

Darius was dismayed that his plan to mount a cavalry charge had been foiled. There was still time for the Persians to regroup. Alexander, seeing a shift in the Persian formation and a momentary weakness, charged with his bodyguards straight at the section where Darius stood. Darius fled with his entourage, and the battle swiftly disintegrated into a rout. Estimated casualties range from 40,000 for the Persians to a mere 500 for the Macedonians. Darius managed to elude Alexander, but was killed by one of his own generals; thus ending the Persian dynasty that began with **Cyrus** (sigh-rus) in the sixth century BC and was, for two centuries, the largest empire in the Western world.

Alexander at the Temple of Amun

Everyone knows that **Rome** was not built in a day, but the city came close to losing its dominance in Italy in one terrible summer afternoon. Rome had entered into a series of wars with a new rival, the city-state of **Carthage**, on the northern coast of Africa. The two city-states fought relentlessly against one another and in the **Second Punic War (223-202 BC)** the Carthaginians sent a remarkable leader, **Hannibal Barca (247?-183? BC)**, to fight in Italy.

Hannibal led his men and elephants from Carthaginian Spain, across the **Alps** and into Italy in the spring of 218 BC. He and his men (few of the elephants survived the trip) emerged exhausted from their march. The Romans thought they would easily defeat the weakened Carthaginians. Instead, the tactical genius of Hannibal and the fighting qualities of his men (Carthaginians, Spanish tribesmen, Gauls and others) led to one surprising victory after another against the larger Roman armies.

In the spring of 216 BC, the Roman **Senate** sent a large army forth under the leadership of two consuls: **Lucius Aemilius Paulus (228-160 BC)** and **Terentius Varro**. The Roman army of 80,000 infantry and 7,000 cavalry encountered Hannibal's 40,000 infantry and 10,000 cavalry at **Cannae** (kan'e) on the north bank of the Ofanto River between Canosa and Barletta, in southern Italy.

Led by Varro, the Romans planned a simple, straightforward battle. Fighting on an open plain (not the swamps and forests

Hannibal had used to good effect in the past), the Romans would advance, employing both numbers and superior discipline to overwhelm the foe. It was a battle plan that had worked many times, against many of Rome's enemies. Hannibal drew up a complicated plan that called for **double envelopment** (encirclement) that would trap the Romans.

As the battle began, Hannibal's cavalrymen (many of them Spanish tribesmen) defeated the Roman cavalry, thus winning on the flanks. The main body of Roman infantry, fighting in its famous **legionnaire** formation, was pushing Hannibal's infantry backwards. At a crucial moment, Hannibal's cavalry appeared on both flanks and then made its way to the Roman rear to completely encircle them. What had begun as a straightforward battle turned into a nightmare for the Romans. They were jammed in so tightly that many of them could not swing their swords. Some 8,000 Romans managed to fight their way out of the trap, but the great majority of men (at least 50,000) died that day on the field at Cannae. Hannibal had not only won a great victory, but demonstrated a strategy for complete victory that generals and tacticians would seek to duplicate for two thousand years to come.

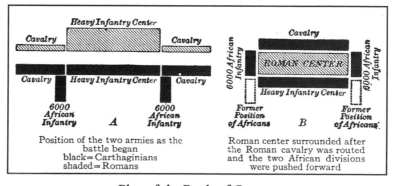

Plan of the Battle of Cannae

15

Hannibal

To the surprise of many of his men, **Hannibal (247?-183? BC)** did not march on Rome in the aftermath of **Cannae** (see no. 8). Lacking siege weapons, he instead tried to persuade other Italian city-states to join in alliance with him against **Rome**. While Hannibal waited, Rome fought against him on another front. Roman armies went to Spain to fight the Carthaginians, who were led by Hannibal's brother, **Hasdrubal Barca**. After several years of campaigning in Spain, the Romans managed to conquer most of the province. Hasdrubal fought his way past the Romans, and made a desperate march in the footsteps of his older brother, across the **Alps** and into the north of Italy.

Hasdrubal sent six messengers to Hannibal, to inform his brother that he was coming. The mounted messengers were captured by a Roman foraging party and thus the Roman Senate soon learned the location and size of Hasdrubal's army, while Hannibal himself knew nothing. Roman Consul **Claudius Nero** marched north with 7,000 hand-picked men to join forces with the army that was already jockeying for position against Hasdrubal and his troops. The battle took place south of the **Metaurus River**, near the present-day village of Saint Angelo, Italy.

Hasdrubal was surprised by the appearance of such a large army, which equaled the size of his own. He made his battle plans quickly, without knowing the terrain or the whereabouts of his brother and the main Carthaginian army. He aligned his Spanish troops on his right, his Ligurians in the center and the Gauls on his left. A steep ravine prevented the Romans from attacking the Carthaginian left, therefore, Nero led several **cohorts**, or legion sections, of Roman infantry south and attacked the unsuspecting Spanish troops on the Carthaginan right. Hasdrubal's elephants had panicked and were useless in the fighting in the center. Seeing the defeat of the Spanish troops on their left, the center-holding Ligurians gave way, and the battle was soon lost. Hasdrubal, in despair, rode his horse deliberately into a Roman cohort and was killed.

Several days later, Hannibal was shown the head of his deceased brother, thrown into the Carthaginian camp by a Roman horseman. At that moment, it is reported, Hannibal knew the end had come to his hope for a lasting victory against Rome.

As **Hannibal's (247?-183? BC)** strength declined following the loss of his brother **Hasdrubal Barca** at the **Metaurus River** (see no. 9), Rome found new ways to strike against Carthage. A young leader of the Roman army, **Publius Cornelius Scipio (237-183 BC)**, later known as **Afrikanus**, had studied Hannibal's tactics for years, and landed over 40,000 Roman troops in Carthage. In response, Carthage negotiated a temporary armistice with Rome, and during that armistice Hannibal and his men sailed from Italy back to North Africa. The stage was set for a conclusive battle between the Carthaginian mastermind and the Roman general who to some extent had copied Hannibal's battle tactics.

Zama (za'mu) was an open plain, set in present-day Zowareen, 60 miles southwest of Tunis. Hannibal brought 45,000 infantry, 3,000 cavalry and 20 elephants to the battle. This was a force far larger than the one he had brought out of Italy, but many of his men were new recruits, not veterans of 20 years of campaigning. By contrast, Scipio had 45,000 men, most of whom were veterans, and he had the assistance of **Numidian** horsemen who had an old grievance against Carthage.

Hannibal drew his forces up in four distinct lines. First, came the elephants, intended to strike fear into the enemy. Second, came mercenary shock troops, whose loyalties were questionable. Third, came militia troops, hastily recruited from Carthage itself. His fourth and final line of men were the 20,000

Publius Cornelius Scipio

veterans he had brought from Italy.

Scipio altered the traditional Roman legion format for the battle. He created open lines between **cohorts** and **maniples** (sections of the legions), and mounted a strong force of cavalry on his right wing. The move must have amused Hannibal since he had used it against the Romans at **Cannae** (see no. 8).

The battle began with the charge of Hannibal's elephants. The Romans blew trumpets at them and opened gaps between the cohorts in order to let the elephants run harmlessly through. Scipio's cavalry then charged and routed the Carthaginian horsemen. Both cavalry groups left the field temporarily. The battle settled into an infantry conflict between the Roman legions and the mix of men Hannibal had brought to the battlefield. The fighting was fierce. Although the Romans overwhelmed the second and third lines of the Carthaginian forces, Hannibal's fourth line-- his veterans--held firm. However, at a critical time in the battle, the Roman and Numidian horsemen returned to the field and executed a double envelopment maneuver on Hannibal, very nearly like what he had done at Cannae. From that point on the issue was never in doubt, although the Carthaginians fought desperately. Hannibal managed to escape from the battle with a handful of men, but 20,000 Carthaginians lost their lives on the field at Zama. Carthage had no choice, but to submit to the terms of Scipio, which ended the **Second Punic War**.

17

Roman Victory

Rome continued to gain strength in the years after the **Battle of Zama** (see no. 10). Having subdued **Hannibal (247?-183? BC)** and Carthage, Rome turned eastward and became embroiled in three wars against the Kingdom of Macedonia. Macedon had been the launching ground for **Alexander the Great (356-323 BC)** and his incredible conquests in the Middle East and Asia, and the kingdom retained a strong military tradition. The Macedonian system of fighting was centered on the **phalanx**, composed of a large block of men, marching and fighting together, usually using heavy spears that were as much as 12 feet long. This wall of spears had overwhelmed and defeated the Persians and had remained the most formidable fighting unit in Greece, Macedonia and the Middle East. Now, however, the phalanx came up against the Roman legion and cohort.

The Roman legion (usually 6,000 men strong) marched and fought in unison, much as the phalanx did. There were two important differences: first, the legion could be broken up into smaller groups, or cohorts, and second, the Romans relied on the short sword more than the spear. The phalanx and legion collided along the banks of the **Aeson River** on the western shore of the **Gulf of Thessalonika**. King **Perseus** of Macedon was in command of 40,000 infantry and 4,000 cavalry. Half of his infantrymen were grouped into a solid, block-like phalanx. His Roman opponent, **Lucius Aemilius Paulus (228-160 BC)**, had brought four Roman legions and their auxiliaries, roughly 25,000 men, to the battlefield.

The fighting began with a minor skirmish along the river. As both sides sent reinforcements, it became a full-scale battle waged between the two armies. At first the Macedonian phalanx used the size and bulk of its formation to push the Romans backward. As the two groups of men reached a large patch of uneven ground, the phalanx became disordered, and the Macedonians had to pause. The Romans counterattacked, and fighting on uneven terrain, began to prevail. They broke into cohorts and sliced their way into the phalanx. In close quarters, the Macedonians found their long spears of little use, while the Romans were able to use their short swords to deadly effect.

What had begun as a test of strength between two armies became a complete rout. By the end of the day, 20,000 Macedonian soldiers were killed or wounded and another 10,000 taken prisoner. By contrast, the Romans reported only 500 men killed or wounded. Such a lopsided affair could only have resulted from a meeting between two different tactical units of battle. The legion became the standard tactical unit, and Rome gained de facto control over both Macedon and Greece.

Every country has a national hero, or set of heroes. In some cases, the hero arises from a gallant, losing cause. Such is the case with the French and **Vercingetorix** (vur- sinje-turiks) **(died 45? BC)** king of the **Arverni** tribe, and leader of all the **Gauls** against the power of Rome.

Around 58 BC, **Julius Caesar (100-44 BC)** led Roman legions into Germany and Gaul (present-day France). A brilliant military leader, Caesar defeated his enemies through keen strategies, a willingness to take risks, and the dogged persistence of his men. Although Gaul was divided into tribes, Vercingetorix managed to persuade most of the tribes to stand with him against Caesar. A charismatic leader, Vercingetorix knew he stood a chance of defeating Caesar as long as he could discipline and control his men. Known for their courage and individuality, the Gallic warriors had little patience for sustained warfare.

The Gauls won the first battle; they successfully defended the fortress of **Gergovia** against a Roman attack. When the two armies met in an open field, the Gallic horsemen panicked at the appearance of Germanic horsemen whom Caesar had hired and brought across the Rhine River. Vercingetorix brought his discouraged army (70,000 strong) to the fortress of **Alesia**, near present-day Dijon, France.

Caesar pursued with 50,000 to 60,000 Roman soldiers. He realized that capturing the stronghold would be too costly. He instructed his men (who always brought pickaxes and shovels as well as swords) to build a wall around the city, intending to starve out Vercingetorix's forces. When Caesar heard that a relief army was being recruited throughout Gaul, he had his men build a second set of walls, completely around the first ring. The inner ring of walls was 11 miles in circumference; the outer set of walls was 14 miles around. When the huge relief army (some historians estimate it was around 250,000 men) arrived, it found the Romans safely ensconced within two sets of fortifications.

The Gauls attacked the Romans from both sides. Vercingetorix made desperate attacks on the inner set of walls while the relief army assailed the outer set of walls. Three times the Gauls sought to break the Roman fortifications and failed. The relief army, which was composed of farmers rather than soldiers, broke into pieces and dispersed.

Vercingetorix surrendered in person to Caesar and was taken to Rome and executed. Rome dominated Gaul for the next 300 years. Today French is referred to as one of the "Romance" languages, a tribute to Roman influence.

Vercingetorix surrenders to Caesar

Two years after winning the **Battle of Alesia** (see no. 12), **Julius Caesar (100-44 BC)** went to war against **Gaius Pompey (106-48 BC)**, a rival Roman leader. Caesar and Pompey had been wary collaborators, but Caesar's victories in Britain, Germany, and Gaul, had provoked envy from Pompey. The two men went to battle to determine who would control matters within the city-state of **Rome**.

As Caesar marched across the **Rubicon River** on his way south toward Rome, Pompey fled the city. Pompey and his followers made their way to the east coast of Italy and took ships across the Adriatic Sea to Greece, where they recruited soldiers and built up their forces. Caesar took the opportunity to run affairs in Rome, where he denounced Pompey as an enemy to the state. Caesar then went to Greece and enacted a hide and seek game with Pompey's forces for several months. Pompey was a masterful strategist. He used the mountainous terrain to keep Caesar off balance, and for one year he managed to avoid the direct battle he dreaded. Although Pompey had a larger army (45,000 infantry and 7,000 cavalry to

Caesar crosses the Rubicon

Caesar's 22,000 infantry and 1,000 cavalry), Caesar's successes on the battlefield had intimidated Pompey.

The two armies finally met for a climactic battle in **Thessaly**. The actual site of the battle is uncertain. Many historians believe it took place beside the Enipeus River below Mount Dogantzis (the name **Pharsalia** comes from the nearby town of Palaepharsalus). When the two armies prepared for battle, it became apparent that the right wing of Caesar's army could not stretch long enough to hold that section of the field. Pompey massed all of his 7,000 cavalry on his left flank and sought to win the battle at the outset with an all-out attack on Caesar's exposed right flank. Although this seemed tactically shrewd, it demonstrated how desperate Pompey was. Not trusting that his men could stand against Caesar's forces, he sought to risk everything at the onset.

Anticipating Pompey's action, Caesar created a reserve force of six cohorts of infantry and his Germanic cavalrymen. Leading this force, Caesar stopped the advance of Pompey's cavalry and turned it back. Pompey fled from the battlefield when he saw his attack fail, and Caesar soon ordered an advance along the line. Although they were outnumbered two-to-one, Caesar and his men made short work of their opponents in the hand-to-hand fighting that followed. By the end of the day, Pompey had lost 15,000 men killed or wounded and 24,000 taken prisoner. Pompey escaped from the battlefield and fled to Egypt where he was murdered. Hoping to please Caesar, the leaders of Egypt presented him with the head of Pompey on a plate. The story is that Caesar turned aside and wept at the sight. Caesar went on to become the undisputed master of Rome until he was assassinated in 45 BC, by Romans who feared that he wanted to become king.

In the years following the death of **Julius Caesar (100-44 BC)**, two men came forward to claim his legacy of leadership. The first was **Mark Antony (82-30 BC)**, a notable military leader who had served under Caesar in many battles, and who had become enamored of Caesar's former mistress, **Cleopatra of Egypt (69-30 BC)**. The second was **Gaius Octavian (63 BC-14 AD)**, later known as **Augustus**, Caesar's nephew by adoption. Antony was bold, brash, and courageous. Octavian was careful, cunning and diplomatic. The two men shared a desire to be the leader of the Roman world, which by this time encompassed most of the Mediterranean.

The two men came to an open clash in 33 BC, and Antony left Rome and went to Egypt where he raised both a fleet and supplies for his army. Assisted by Cleopatra, Antony appeared to be in a strong position. However, Octavian was a master of propaganda. He persuaded the Roman Senate that Antony was a traitor to Rome and that he intended to make Egypt the center of the Mediterranean. When Octavian sailed from Italy to meet and fight Antony, he had the full resources of the city of Rome behind him.

Octavian landed on the west coast of Greece, where Antony was training his forces. Assisted by his brilliant general **Marcus Vipsanius Agrippa (63-12 BC)**, Octavian was soon able to blockade Antony and Cleopatra from their supply lines. Outmaneuvered, Antony decided upon a straightforward fight to resolve the matter. He might have remained on land and held an advantage since he was a far more experienced soldier than Octavian, but he was persuaded by Cleopatra to risk the matter at sea.

On September 2, 31 BC, Antony and Cleopatra led their combined fleet out of the harbor of **Actium**, with 480 galleys that carried at least 20,000 soldiers. It is unclear whether Antony truly hoped to win the battle or whether he merely wanted to cut his way past the enemy and make his way to Egypt.

The fighting was fierce. Octavian and Agrippa had equipped their ships with machines that hurled rocks at the enemy. As the day progressed, Octavian's forces began to gain the upper hand. Antony ran up a flag that was the signal for his fleet to give up the battle and attempt to escape past the enemy. Antony, Cleopatra, and some forty of their ships managed the feat, but the remainder, some three hundred ships, surrendered to Octavian and Agrippa, as did the rest of Antony's land forces.

Antony and Cleopatra reached Egypt. His spirit defeated, Antony made little effort to resist the invasion of Egypt by Octavian. Both Antony and Cleopatra committed suicide rather than surrender. More cautious than his uncle Julius Caesar had been, Octavian asked only for the title of **Princeps** (First Citizen of Rome). Though he never was called Emperor, he ruled Rome from 30 BC-14 AD and set up the form of one-man government that made Rome into his empire in all but name.

Cleopatra of Egypt

The Battle of Teutoburger Wald

During the rule of **Gaius Octavian (63 BC-14 AD)** (later known as **Augustus**) the boundaries of the Roman Empire reached their greatest extent. Few peoples sought to fight the Roman legions, which had become legendary for their skill and ferocity. It seemed as if **Rome** would dominate the lands around the Mediterranean Sea forever.

One exception to this rule, however, were the Germanic tribes who lived east of the **Rhine River** in Germany. The Germans had fought against the Romans many times, and **Julius Caesar (100-44 BC)** had defeated them repeatedly. Yet the Germans still ruled their own territory, and they intended to keep. Little is known of the Germans during this time because the histories were all written by Romans. What can be gathered indicates that they were a vigorous, warlike people who lived primarily through hunting. Frustrated by the Romans in battle, the Germans finally found an appropriate way to fight against their long-standing enemies.

In 9 AD, **Publius Quintilius Varus** led three Roman legions and their auxiliaries (about 20,000 men, including 1,500 cavalry) to suppress an uprising by German tribes along Rome's northern frontier. The Germans were led by **Arminius**, leader of the **Cheruscan** tribe that masterminded the revolt. Varus led a pursuit of the Germans into the broken and heavily forested area known as the **Teutoburger Wald**, presently known as the Grotenburg, southwest of Detmold, Germany. Violent rainstorms made the going laborious for the Romans.

Varus and his men were suddenly attacked by great numbers of Germans who hurled javelins at them from the cover of the woods. Varus halted, made camp, and fortified his position. Under normal circumstances, this would have been enough to repel any attack, but the Germans had inspired leadership from Arminius. Another downpour of rain disorganized the Roman lines, and the Germans came forward in a straight assault. The Roman cavalry fled from the scene, and the infantry was compelled to fight in terrain that was ill-suited to the tactics of the legion.

Had Varus been another Caesar, the Romans might have prevailed. Lacking such brilliant leadership, the Roman troops disintegrated into small groups that were overwhelmed by their foes. By nightfall, the Roman army was nearly exterminated. Those Romans who were captured, were sacrificed to the Germanic gods.

16. MASADA
72-73 AD

Few countries of the Mediterranean world were able to resist the Roman impulse toward conquest and domination. One group who succumbed to **Rome**, still maintained their dignity. They were the **Hebrews** of ancient **Israel**. The land itself had been taken over by the Romans in the first century AD, but there remained a strong movement among the **Jews** (the **Zealot movement**) to remove the foreigners and bring back holy rule to Israel.

The Jewish rebellion against Rome (66-70 AD) was a costly failure. Roman legions took **Jerusalem** and dispersed many of the Jews who were living there. A group of Zealots, however, held out against these defeats, assuring their fellow Jews that retribution was not far off. In 72 AD, the Zealots, led by **Eleazer ben Yair**, found their last remaining stronghold on the fortified mountain of **Masada** on the western shore of the Dead Sea.

The Roman leader, **Flavius Silva**, positioned the Tenth Roman legion and its auxiliary troops (about 7,000 men in all) at the foot of the mountain. Although Masada was defended by only 1,000 Jews, the steep cliffs and rocks provided an excellent means of defense, and the Jews were able to hold out against the early Roman assaults. To counter the geographical advantage of his foes, Silva had a 300-foot-high ramp constructed, with a stone platform 75 feet high that was capped by an armored siege tower. Through means of this bulky instrument, the Romans were able to make a breach in the walls of Masada. Even so, the Jews fought back with skill and daring. They built a rampart of timber and earth to seal off the breach, but the Romans soon set fire to it. Eleazer counseled his fellow Jews to take their own lives rather than submit to the tyranny of Rome. When the Romans finally entered the fortress, they found that 960 Jews had committed suicide, leaving only two women and five children who had concealed themselves. The Roman losses were light, but the Jews had gained a moral victory in their defense and defeat.

Roman camp near Masada, still visible

The Roman Empire lost some of its strength during the fourth century AD. The city of **Rome** itself became less important and the city of **Constantinople** (present-day Istanbul, built where the Black Sea connects with the Mediterranean) became the center of the empire. Around 370 AD, the Emperor **Valens** (328?-378) allowed large numbers of the **Goths**, (a warlike tribe from east central Europe) to cross the boundary of the empire and settle within Roman territory. Roman tax collectors began to squeeze all they could from the Goths, and by 378 AD there was a full-scale revolt by these "barbarian" people living within the empire.

The Emperor Valens led the Roman army. He brought 40,000 infantry and 20,000 cavalry from Constantinople north to the present-day border between Greece and Bulgaria. The Goths had collected an army of 100,000 men, half cavalry and half infantry. These numbers did not dismay the Roman leaders,

Goths and a Roman soldier

as hundreds of years of military history had shown that the Roman legion was almost invincible when it fought in the open. Many of the Goths had served as mercenaries in the Roman armies, and they were also much better armed than their predecessors had been in the days of **Julius Caesar (100-44 BC)** or **Gaius Octavian (Augustus) (63 BC-14 AD)**.

Fritigern, leader of the Goths, planned his strategy well. The Gothic infantry was protected by a wagon fort while the cavalry waited in wooded areas close to the field. When the Romans approached, Fritigern met them with terms of a truce. Some of the Roman soldiers broke the truce, and the battle began while the Roman army was still coming into formation.

At first the battle was an even struggle between two well-matched forces. The Romans assailed the wagon fort, while the Goths defended it, using arrows and darts. The element of surprise lay with the Gothic cavalry, which suddenly appeared on the field and routed its Roman counterpart. Large numbers of Gothic warriors, both mounted and on foot, surrounded the Roman army and began a fight of attrition. Lacking horsemen, the Romans could not fight their way out of the trap. As evening approached, the Emperor withdrew to a peasant's cottage, which was soon set on fire by the Goths. Valens died, and with him the last hopes of his army. At least 40,000 Romans, two-thirds of the army, died on the battlefield.

Adrianople was the greatest loss suffered to that date by the Roman Empire. A tribe of warlike peoples had overwhelmed a sizeable Roman army in broad daylight on an open plain. The battle proclaimed the new ascendancy of the "barbarian" peoples and foreshadowed the complete sack of Rome itself by the Goths in 410 AD.

18. CHALONS-SUR-MARNE
451 AD

The eternal city of **Rome** endured a ferocious sack by the Goths in 410 AD, but continued, in title, to be the capital of the Roman Empire. During the decade of the 440s, a new enemy arose to challenge what was left of the empire. This foe was **Attila (406-453)**, leader of the **Huns**, a people from Central Asia, who had defeated every other tribe from their homeland to Europe. Atilla was intent upon reducing the Roman Empire. Balked by the strong walls that surrounded **Constantinople**, he turned toward **Gaul** (present-day France) in 451 AD.

All of Roman Europe trembled at the mention of Atilla. The savagery of his warriors was legendary. Some historians have mentioned that hydrogen bombs are not any more fearsome to twentieth century Americans than Atilla was to fifth century Europeans.

Atilla marched his horde of warriors, estimated at anywhere between 100,000 and 300,000 in number, across the **Rhine River** and began to sack many of the towns and cities of eastern Gaul.

Two leaders emerged to oppose the Huns. **Flavius Aetius (396?-454)**, master of the Roman Soldiers, entered into a temporary alliance with **Theodoric**, king of the **Visigothic** tribe. Although the Visigoths had sacked Rome in 410 AD, they presented a less fearsome challenge than did the Huns.

The Roman-Visigothic army met the Huns at **Chalons**, about 18 miles north of Troyes in present-day France. The size of the combined army is unknown, but it was probably larger than that of the Huns. Atilla opened the battle, sending his best men straight against the center part of the enemy's line. The Huns smashed through the center and turned on the right wing of the foe, which was held by the Visigoths. Atilla was close to victory, but the left wing of the combined army, made up of Roman soldiers, stood firm. When the

The Battle of Chalons-sur-Marne

Gothic cavalry launched a counterattack, a ferocious hand-to-hand battle ensued, with soldiers on both sides being cut off from orders from their superiors. In this desperate melee, the Romans and Visigoths fared better than the Huns, and Atilla was eventually forced to order a retreat. Theodoric was killed in the fighting, and Aetius did not exploit his victory, which left Atilla free to menace Europe again the following year. Although Chalons was not an outright victory for the Romans and Visigoths, it did permit Roman civilization to endure in Europe, long after the passing of Atilla and his ferocious armies.

The arid and inhospitable peninsula of Arabia (known today as Saudi Arabia) played a very small part in world history until the coming of the prophet **Mohammed (570-632)**. Born in the merchant town of **Mecca**, Mohammed was visited by the angel **Gabriel** who ordered him to "recite" the word of **Allah**. Within a few years, Mohammed became the leader of a new faith, the Muslims, whose very name declared their submission to Allah. The Muslims believed that "There is no God but Allah, and Mohammed is his Prophet."

Mohammed was not well received by his fellow townspeople of Mecca, who were pagans. He fled from the city in 622 AD and found refuge in the city of **Medina**, 210 miles to the north. There he gathered his true followers and began a war against the rich caravans that went to Mecca. His great enemy was **Abu Sufyan**, leader of the **Koriesh** tribe in Arabia. In 624, Mohammed won the **Battle of Badr**, but in 625, was defeated at the **Battle of Ohod**. Following this defeat, Mohammed retreated to Medina. This retrenchment brought about a full-scale attack on Medina by the Koriesh tribesmen under Abu Sufyan.

In 627, Sufyan brought 10,000 of his followers north and laid siege to Medina. The town was defended by Mohammed, at the lead of 3,000 of his most devout followers. The Muslims dug a trench completely around the town and repulsed every attack by the Koriesh. After twenty days of intermittent fighting, the Koriesh withdrew, leaving Mohammed in control of his adopted city.

In 628, Mohammed and his adversaries agreed to the **Treaty of Hudaybiya**, which granted the Muslims the right to make pilgrimages to Mecca. When this treaty was broken in 629, Mohammed led his followers on the 210-mile journey south to Mecca and laid siege to his former hometown. In January 630, Mohammed and his men stormed into the town and won most of the inhabitants to the Muslim faith. Mohammed is reported to have destroyed some 360 pagan idols. By the time of his death, he had stamped out paganism in Arabia and created a unified force of Muslim warriors who would go forth to confound much of the former Greek, Persian, and Roman worlds in the century to come.

The small conflicts that gave control of Arabia to Mohammed were of immense importance. They opened the way for a faith and an approach to life and warfare that took root in the Middle East, and became one of the most practiced religions in the world.

Map of ARABIA and adjacent countries

ASIA MINOR
Fertile land.....
Sandy desert....
Steppe desert....
Mountain ridges
Mediterranean
Jerusalem
Damascus
Petra
EGYPT
Persian Gulf
Medina
Red Sea
Mecca
ARABIA
Yemen
ABYSSINIA
J.F.H.

Constantinople, Seraglid Point

The defense of the city was in the hands of Emperor **Leo III (680?-741)**. A capable soldier, Leo massed the Byzantine fleet to prevent the Muslim ships from passing the city and entering the Black Sea. When the Muslims tried to force the issue, they were defeated by a combination of Byzantine seamanship and the use of **Greek fire**, a combination of sulfur, quicklime, naphtha and seawater that was catapulted at the Muslim ships. Having successfully defended the water route past Constantinople, Leo then directed the defense by land.

In terms of numbers, the Muslims were in an advantageous position. They had some 80,000 men, while Leo had only half that number. The winter of 717 to 718 was colder than usual, and many of the Egyptian and Arab invaders were suffering from the frigid temperatures. To make matters worse for the besiegers, Leo persuaded the kingdom of the **Bulgars** to send a relief army to the area. A battle was fought between the Muslims and Bulgars to the northwest of Constantinople, and some 22,000 of the Arabs lost their lives. In response to this, Maslama ended the siege, concluding twelve months of conflict.

The conquests of **Mohammed (570-632)**, founder of the Islamic religion, and his successors, brought the Muslim world, which believed in **Allah**, into contact and conflict with the **Byzantine** world, which had developed Orthodox Christianity (see no. 19). **Constantinople**, the capital and nerve center of the Byzantine Empire, was attacked and besieged by Muslim warriors from 717 to 718.

Following the death of Mohammed, they had come out of Arabia to conquer all of the **Holy Land** (Jordan, Israel, Lebanon and Syria). In 717 AD, **Maslama**, brother of the caliph of Damascus in Syria, gathered a huge army of 80,000 infantry, supported by a fleet of roughly 800 ships. Maslama laid siege to Constantinople, the greatest prize any Arab conqueror could hope to obtain, on August 15, 717.

Six years before the defeat of the Muslim army at **Constantinople** from 717 to 718 (see no. 20), a small Arab force made its way all along the coast of North Africa, crossed at the **Strait of Gibraltar**, and proceeded to conquer all of Visigothic Spain. It seemed quite possible that Arab armies in Spain might move north and join their counterparts fighting against the Byzantines in Asia Minor and at Constantinople. Mindful of this danger, the **Franks**, living in Gaul (present-day France) sought a leader and a new style of fighting with which to resist the Arabs.

Charles Martel (688?-741), also known as **Charles the Hammer**, developed a block-like **phalanx** infantry formed from a militia of Frankish veterans that was reminiscent of the one used by the Greeks under **Alexander the Great (356-323 BC)** (see no. 6). Martel kept a close watch on the Pyrenees Mountains that marked the border between France and Spain. In 732, Martel learned of the advance of a large body of Arab troops, most of them on horseback. Some chroniclers state that the Arab leader, **Abderrahman Ibu Abdillah**, brought 80,000 men across the Pyrenees into France; many historians say the number is an exaggeration as he could not have fed such a large body of men.

Martel and his Frankish troops met the Arab/Moorish enemy on the field of **Cenon**, midway between **Tours** and Poitiers. Martel formed his men into a rigid phalanx, using spears and swords to fend off cavalry charges by the enemy. The Arabs were accustomed to fighting forcefully and gaining rapid victory in battle. They had defeated many of their foes through sheer bravado and belief that **Allah** was guiding them in the struggle. Martel's men held strong against the charges by the lightly armed, but highly motivated Arab horsemen. The Arab chroniclers of the battle declare that it lasted for two days, while some of the Christian records claim that it went on for seven days. Martel's foot soldiers were able to withstand the charges, and the Arabs eventually withdrew; leaving behind the booty they had picked up from their conquests in southern France. Ibu Abdillah was killed in the fighting, and his men retreated to Spain. Although some raids would be conducted in the future against the coast of southern France (present-day Riviera), no major invasion would again be launched by the Arabs. Martel's victory ensured that there would not be a Muslim takeover of central Europe.

The Battle of Tours

The most decisive battle in English history was fought on an autumn day in East Sussex, in lower England. The contest was between the Norman warriors of **Duke William of Normandy (1027-1087)**, also known as **William the Bastard**, for his illegitimate birth, and the **Anglo-Saxon** soldiers of King **Harold II (1022?- 1066)** of England.

Harold was crowned king in 1066, over the heir apparent Duke William. William contested the throne and assembled an army of 8,000 to 10,000 men to invade England. William's army had to wait in Normandy, on the coast of France, for a favorable wind and tide in order to cross the Channel. During that same time, King Harold was forced to march north and fight against an invasion by Norwegians in the area of York. Harold defeated his Scandinavian foes and then countermarched his men swiftly to London, to meet the arrival of Williams' ships. William's army had landed on the English shore at Pevensey and marched to **Hastings**, where they were met by Harold and his troops.

Harold brought 2,000 house carls (the troops of his household) and 5,500 militia troops to the battle. William had the same number of men, but his men had the advantage of being rested. Harold's men had marched and countermarched some 500 miles in the two weeks prior to the battle. In addition, the Normans had a clear superiority in horsemen.

The battle took place on an uneven stretch of land, with Harold and his men holding the higher ground. The Anglo-Saxons formed a shield wall and defended it against numerous attacks by both the cavalry and archers of the Norman army. After one failed attack, it was reported that Duke William had fallen. To restore confidence in his men, William quickly removed his helmet so his men could see his face; he rode up and down the ranks of his

The Battle of Hastings

army to assure his men that he was alive. Medieval armies often panicked or dispersed following the death of their leader.

The struggle went on all day. Toward evening, King Harold was struck in the eye by an arrow and later killed in hand-to-hand fighting. His death greatly discouraged his men, and William took advantage of the moment to launch an all-out attack upon the shield wall. Finally, the Normans succeeded in breaking through, winning the battle, and ending the fight. Each side is believed to have lost 2,000 men.

With the death of Harold, William had no other rival to speak of. He marched north and was crowned King of England in London on Christmas Day 1066. People began to call him **William the Conqueror**. Anglo-Saxon England passed into the hands of Norman rule, a rule that would leave a long and definite imprint upon English society, culture and politics. The centralization of power, success in architecture, city-building, law and government that we presently associate with England had their roots in the Norman conquest of 1066.

The Muslim empire that had menaced **Constantinople** from 717 to 718 (see no. 20) and was defeated at **Tours** in 732 (see no. 21), lost its energy around 1000 AD. It was revitalized by the appearance of the **Seljuk Turks**, a large clan of Central Asian warriors, who had captured **Baghdad** (the capital of present-day Iraq) in 1035, and converted to Islam. These new soldiers of the Crescent soon made renewed attacks upon the **Byzantine Empire**.

The main strength of the Byzantine Empire was its control of Asia Minor, present-day Turkey. From there, the empire drew its best food products and its most committed soldiers. When the Seljuk Turks, led by their famous commander **Alp Arslan**, advanced on **Armenia** and threatened the eastern part of Asia Minor, the Byzantines were compelled to respond.

Byzantine Emperor **Romanus Diogenes IV (died 1072)** led his army to the city of **Manzikert** in eastern Asia Minor and retook that city from the Turks. Learning of the advance of the Byzantine army, Alp Arslan brought his main body of troops (roughly 40,000 men) from Syria to the area around Manzikert. The two armies collided in what became one of the most fateful battles in the history of the Middle East.

Although they were ferocious fighters, the Turks had little military organization. Their army was divided into warrior groups of mounted archers who were better at skirmishing with and harassing an enemy than at a straight on fight. Although the Byzantine army was made up of professional soldiers, there was considerable disloyalty in the ranks.

The Turks opened the battle, sending forth their horse-archers. Romanus ordered his infantry forward, and his foot soldiers pushed the archers and the main body of Turks back as the afternoon progressed. The Byzantines were also forced to pull back due to a lack of water supplies. When they did, the Turks set upon them in an all-out attack. The Byzantines could have held their ground had not one of Romanus' generals, **Andronicus Ducas**, betrayed the emperor's cause by failing to turn his column around to confront the enemy. As a result, the main body of Byzantine troops was completely cut off from its camp and surrounded by the Seljuk Turks.

Given these odds, the Byzantines had no chance to cut their way out. Thousands of men died where they stood, and Romanus was brought before Alp Arslan as a prisoner. The battle gave control of Asia Minor to the Turks and spurred the crusading movement which began 20 years later.

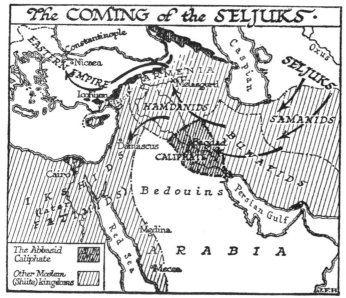

The COMING of the SELJUKS.

Following the Turkish victory at **Manzikert** (see no. 23), the Byzantine Emperor pleaded with the Pope in Rome to send soldiers to help defend the Holy Land. In 1095, **Pope Urban II (born 1053?)** preached a sermon at Clermont, France, imploring the knights of Western Christendom to cease fighting with one another and march to the Holy Land to recapture **Jerusalem.**

Crusaders on their way to Palestine

Two groups set off to reclaim Jerusalem: the **Peasants' Crusade** and the **Knights' Crusade.** The first phase consisted of a peasant army of 30,000 men led by a charismatic preacher named **Peter the Hermit.** These untrained warriors were caught in an ambush by the Turks in the mountains of Asia Minor and many of them were killed. The second group, the Knights' Crusade, was better supplied and equipped in weaponry and armor. Over 30,000 men came forward, hoping to gain wealth. Many of the leaders were knights of Normandy, men whose fathers had fought with **William the Conqueror (1027-1087)** at the **Battle of Hastings** (see no. 22)

The army of knights went to Constantinople, crossed over into Asia Minor, and made their way down the coast to Jerusalem. There were some notable battles along the way, particularly the siege of **Antioch** in 1097, but the crowning phase of the campaign was the battle for Jerusalem in the summer of 1099.

Pope Urban had described the Holy Land as a place of milk and honey. The crusaders found it otherwise, especially since the Turks poisoned all of the wells within a twenty-mile radius of Jerusalem. The crusaders reached the city on June 15, 1099 and started a siege. One especially devout crusader told his fellows about a dream that told him they would not capture the city until they had purified their hearts. For three days, the crusaders marched around the walls of Jerusalem, chanting prayers for forgiveness and absolution for their sins. They made a ferocious attack upon the city at the end of the rite.

The crusaders used two siege towers to attack the ramparts. The Turks used oil and boiling water against the attackers, who, in their turn, employed flame-tipped arrows against the defenders. After hours of fighting, the crusaders broke open one of the gates and entered the city. There followed one of the most horrendous massacres in the long military history of the Holy Land. Some accounts state that for three days time, the crusaders ran amok in the city, killing every Muslim and Turk. Estimates of the number killed ran as high as 70,000.

After the battle and conquest, Jerusalem became the capital of a new crusader kingdom. As a result, Turkish oils, carpets, spices, and other luxuries found their way from the Holy Land to Europe, increasing the desire for the goods among the Europeans and creating a new class of merchant traders.

Jerusalem

The Christian kingdoms that were created in the Holy Land after the **Battle of Jerusalem** (see no. 24) lasted until the last quarter of the twelfth century. Stone castles still stand today where the crusaders left their mark in the Middle East. **Yusuf Salah ad-Din (1138-1193)**, better known to Westerners as **Saladin** (sah-la-deen), the ruler of Arab-controlled Egypt, arose to challenge the crusaders.

Born a Kurd (a member of the tribe that has been harassed in modern times by Iraq's **Saddham Hussein**), Saladin became the leader of Muslim Egypt, which had never succumbed to the crusaders. In 1187, he brought an army from Egypt and threatened to take Jerusalem away from the Europeans. His opponent, King **Guy** of Jerusalem, led 1,200 knights and 18,000 men-at-arms out of Jerusalem and into the arid region bordering on the Sea of Galilee.

Saladin rejoiced when he learned that the Christians were marching through the desert toward him. He immediately sent detachments of mounted archers to harass the enemy as they advanced. Saladin, with his back to the Sea of Galilee, had a regular supply of water, while the crusaders did not. King Guy and his men marched through arid

conditions and arrived at the **Horns of Hattin** where they found their way blocked by the main body of Saladin's army. The crusaders camped for the night, during which time Saladin's men set fire to the scrub brush around the Christians' encampment, creating smoke and making the desire for water more intense.

The battle lasted the entire day. Despite their precarious position, the crusaders fought with great valor. The **True Cross** (believed to have been the very one upon which **Jesus Christ** was crucified) stood on a hillside as did the battle flag of King Guy. As long as these emblems stood, there appeared to be some hope for the Christian army.

Saladin sent his mounted archers forth to attack his foes. The Muslims were less armored than the Christians, and hand-to-hand fighting often went in favor of the latter. Toward the end of the day, Saladin launched an all-out assault with both cavalry and infantry. The True Cross and King Guy's flag were both captured, as were King Guy and many of his nobles.

Nearly all members of the Christian army had been killed or captured. Saladin spared the life of King Guy, but he had some 200 knights beheaded on the spot. Saladin went on to besiege and accept the surrender of Jerusalem itself on October 2, 1187. Unlike the crusaders who had butchered the civilian population in 1099, Saladin allowed the Christians of Jerusalem to ransom themselves for gold. The battle of the Horns of Hattin gave control of the Holy Land back to the Muslims, who would keep that control until 1917.

While Christians and Muslims fought against each other during the Crusades (see no. 24 and no. 25), a new enemy of both these peoples arose from the steppes of Central Asia. **Temujin**, better known in the west as **Genghis Khan (1167-1227)**, became the leader of the **Mongols** by 1200. He led his fierce Mongol warriors against China, northern India, and then turned his attention to western Asia, bordering on the Holy Land.

Samarkand was an ancient city that had been the capital of Persian and Arab peoples. In 1220, it was the center of the **Kwaewzmian** empire, which occupied the lands between the Middle East (to its west) and the Mongol and Chinese territories (to its east). Genghis Khan decided that a capture of Samarkand would help spread his name.

In June 1220, the Mongols laid siege to the city. Samarkand was defended by a garrison of 110,000 men under the leadership of **Alub Khan**, governor of the city. Genghis Khan brought 120,000 Mongols to the siege; these were men who were hardened through years of fighting many enemies and living on the steppes of Central Asia. They were generally unaccustomed to siege warfare. There was a good possibility that if the garrison could hold out, the Mongols would be forced to disperse due to a lack of forage for their animals. This was always a concern for nomadic fighters, whether they were Huns, Mongols, Seljuk Turks or others.

The Mongols made repeated assaults upon the city. They terrified the inhabitants with their tactics and ferocious appearance, but the city held firm against the attacks. Some of the inhabitants decided that it might be better to work with the invaders rather than to resist them. Hoping for clemency from the Mongols, these people opened a gate for the enemy to ride into the city. Any hope they had for mercy was lost. Genghis Khan and his men entered in a fury; they were used to swifter victories. They rampaged through the city, killing both soldiers and civilians at will. Alub Khan managed to fight his way out of Samarkand with 1,000 horsemen; they were the only survivors of what had been the jeweled city of Central Asia.

Genghis Khan had been correct in estimating that his victory would spread his name throughout the world. The battle greatly extend the Mongol empire, which soon showed signs of expanding into the Middle East and Europe.

Genghis Khan

Genghis Khan's (1167-1227) son and grandson followed him to the throne of the new Mongol empire. One of the greatest periods of Mongol expansion came during the rule of his grandson, **Mangu Khan**, who reigned from 1251 to 1259.

Mangu Khan sent his younger brother, **Hulagu**, to conquer areas in the Muslim-controlled Middle East. The Muslims, whether Arabians or Seljuk Turks, had controlled the key cities of **Baghdad**, **Damascus**, **Jerusalem**, and **Alexandria**, ever since the original Arab conquests during the eighth century. Hulagu was seeking to end a domination that had lasted for some 400 years.

The Mongols encircled and then besieged Baghdad during the winter of 1258. The defenders of the city were led by **Mustasim**, last of the original line of the **Abbassid** caliphs. These men had been at the center of the Muslim world for four centuries, and their word was law in religious and secular matters.

The Arab defenders had a long and illustrious military tradition, and the city itself was well protected by walls and ditches. Baghdad could not withstand the fury of the Mongol assault. Hardened by years of fighting in Central Asia, China, and the northern reaches of India, the Mongols burst into the city on February 15, 1258. The slaughter that followed was horrendous. Thousands of Muslim soldiers and civilians were killed. Mustasim was captured and trampled to death by horses. An old legend in Middle Eastern history is that Hulagu taunted Mustasim with Baghdad gold, asking him why he had not used this wealth to hire more soldiers. Fresh from the victory, Hulagu pressed on toward Syria and Lebanon.

The Mongol forces under Hulagu easily scattered the forces that sought to resist them in Syria and Lebanon. Upon learning, however, that his older brother, Mangu Khan, had died, Hulagu began a slow and orderly retreat, planning to return to China to participate in the selection of a new Khan. As he pulled back, Hulagu was pursued by **Mameluke** soldiers from Muslim-controlled Egypt. Knowing the fate of their Arab cousins in Baghdad, the **Mamelukes** resolved never to yield to the Mongol conquerors. **Baybars I**, general of the Mamelukes, led an attack on the Mongol rearguard at **Ain Jalut**, near the Sea of Galilee, in September 1260. The Mameluke cavalry cut the rearguard of the Mongols to pieces. The main body of the Mongols reversed direction and entered the battle as well. Ten thousand Mongols were defeated in the battle by 12,000 Mamelukes. This was the first loss that the Mongols had suffered in the Western region.

Baghdad

The Mongol empire reached its greatest physical extent during the reign of **Kublai Khan (1216-1294)**. This Khan, who was visited by **Marco Polo (1254?-1324)**, presided over more of the Earth's surface than any man since **Alexander the Great (356-323 BC)**. He is best known in military history for his most significant defeat: the **Battles of Hakata Bay** in 1274 and 1281.

One of the few countries that had maintained freedom from the Mongols was Japan. Korea fell under the influence of the Mongols during Kublai Khan's early years as emperor. Kublai Khan amassed a large army and fleet to attack Japan. A joint **Mongol-Korean** fleet crossed the Sea of Japan and captured the islands of **Tsushima** and **Iki**. The troops made a landing at Hakata Bay in northern Kyushu in November. Better armed, and more disciplined than their Japanese opponents, the Mongols easily held the beachhead. Seeing that a major storm was brewing, the Mongols and Koreans returned to their ships and attempted to sail home. A tremendous typhoon struck the fleet and 200 ships were sunk, with a loss of 13,000 lives. A combination of determined resistance and the fortunes of the weather had saved Japan.

Kublai Khan was furious over this debacle. In 1281 he sent another fleet and army to Japan. The Mongol and Chinese ships converged on the island of Iki, where the Japanese engaged them in ship-to-ship fighting. The smaller size of the Japanese vessels enabled them to outmaneuver the Mongols and to win numerous small victories on the water. The fighting went on intermittently between June 23 to August 14, 1281, until

Japanese battle Mongol warriors

another typhoon struck. The fleet that Kublai Khan had sent across the Sea of Japan was almost entirely wrecked on the Japanese coast. Nearly half of the Mongol and Chinese troops drowned; those who survived and made their way to the beaches were massacred by the Japanese. From that time on, there was no question that Japan would remain independent of the Mongol empire. The Japanese have referred to a **Kamikaze** or **Divine Wind** as an element in their favor.

England and Scotland share the same island, but the two peoples, English and Scottish, have always been quite distinct from one another. During the reign of King **Edward I** of England, from 1272 to 1307, England managed to turn Scotland into more or less a territory of England. This changed when **Robert the Bruce (1274-1329)**, Scottish leader and patriot, challenged the English on the field of **Bannockburn**.

Robert the Bruce came from a long line of distinguished Scottish nobles. He had fought against the English numerous times, but had been defeated again and again. The English and Welsh were masters of the longbow, and they had scattered the Scots in many battles.

King **Edward II (1284-1327)** marched north with 17,000 infantrymen and 1,000 cavalry. His object was to relieve **Stirling Castle**, which was under siege by a Scottish army of 9,000 infantry and 500 cavalry, commanded by Robert the Bruce. Robert the Bruce was pleased that the English were committing themselves to a decisive battle on Scottish soil.

On the morning of June 24, Robert the Bruce divided his men into four **schiltrons** of pikemen, each of which resembled a Macedonian **phalanx** (a wall of swords and spears). This Scottish formation had been developed during the revolt led by **William Wallace (1270?-1305)** twenty years earlier, when Scottish foot soldiers had unhorsed English knights through the use of long wood staves. King Edward II sent his cavalry in first to attack the schiltrons. Although the English horsemen were renowned for their skill, they were unable to make a dent in the solid Scottish schiltrons. Their attack blocked the way of the English archers, who might otherwise have succeeded in killing the Scots.

To get a clear field of fire, the archers moved out to the right flank and unleashed a dangerous hail of arrows at the Scots. Bruce then ordered his cavalry in, which charged at the English archers. At that moment, the Scottish schiltrons made a deliberate move against the main body of English troops. Seeing the failure of their attack and the approach of the schiltrons, large sections of the English army simply broke and fled, leaving the field to the Scots. By the day's end, the English lost over 1,000 infantry, 22 barons, and 68 knights, and many others were killed during the pursuit that followed. The Scots lost two knights and 500 infantrymen. The battle gave true independence to Scotland and established Robert the Bruce as both king and national hero of his land.

Wallace leading a charge

During the late Middle Ages, England and France fought for over one hundred years against each other. One of the first battles was that of **Crecy**, fought in northeastern France between the English army led by King **Edward III (1312-1377)**, and the French army led by King **Philip VI (1293-1350)**.

King Edward invaded France with a small elite force of 10,000 men (including 5,500 archers, most of whom used the longbow). He marched along the northeast coast of France, waiting for a challenge from the French army.

At that time, most feudal European monarchs did not maintain a standing army. They sent out heralds to summon the knights of their vassals when there was a need to fight. It took some time for the French army to assemble, but it presented a truly formidable force. King Philip mustered 30,000 men total: 6,000 infantry, 10,000 men-at-arms, and 14,000 militia, more than enough to destroy the English invaders. The French caught up with the English at the field of Crecy, 10 miles north of Abbeville, in Picardy, France. The English had prepared the battlefield with care. They had dug potholes to trap the charging French knights and deployed their troops in a way that placed their archers on the flanks of the men-at-arms.

The French army arrived in a piecemeal fashion; some knights arriving at the field, then a pause, followed by the arrival of another group of knights. The battle began with an exchange of arrows between the English long bowmen and **Genoese crossbowmen**, hired by the French. The crossbow released a mighty dart, but the rate at which it could be fired was extremely slow compared to the longbow. The English cleared away the archers of the French and then concentrated their fire against the enemy's knights. The French knights were so anxious to charge that

The Battle of Crecy

they moved without coordination between their units. Hundreds of French knights were trapped in the potholes that had been prepared for them, or were cut down by the longbow, which had accuracy of up to 300 yards.

Each section of French knights that arrived on the battlefield charged the enemy and was shattered by a combination of arrows, potholes, and English swords. Around midnight, King Philip withdrew his remaining forces from the battlefield. The French lost 1,542 nobles and knights and around 10,000 troops. The English losses numbered at 100 men killed or wounded. This was the greatest single day's loss ever sustained by a European army in the Middle Ages to date. It showed that infantry with a strong position, supported by archers, could defeat the best knights in Europe. King Edward then went on to besiege the French town of **Calais**. In that siege, the English used **cannon** for the first time in European warfare.

The Battle of Agincourt

The **Hundred Years' War** (1330-1453) between England and France raged on as the fourteenth century yielded to the start of the fifteenth. In England, a new king, **Henry V (1387-1422)**, decided he wanted to end the matter by conquering France. During the summer of 1415, he brought 7,000 men from England to Normandy, where he captured the city of **Harfleur**. King Henry then marched his small army toward Calais, on the northeast coast of France, intending to spend the winter there.

During the summer **Charles D'Albret**, the Constable of France, raised an army of 25,000, which included 22,000 mounted knights and 3,000 crossbow men. D'Albret brought this large and impressive army north and caught up with the English east of the village of **Agincourt**, between the cities of Abbeville and Calais.

Given the disparity between the two armies, D'Albret expected the English to surrender to him. Henry V rejected the heralds that D'Albret sent and dared the French to fight to the death. D'Albret saw that it would be wisest to surround the English and bring about their surrender from a lack of food. This calm approach was not palatable to the more ambitious of his knights; they wanted to attack and destroy the enemy. D'Albret commenced the battle on October 25, known as **St. Crispin's Day**.

The English had taken up position across the narrowest part of the road between Agincourt and Tramcourt. They deployed their archers on the flanks and protected their center section with a line of iron-tipped stakes. Henry V was instrumental in keeping up the morale of his men; he ceaselessly paced through the lines of his troops assuring them they would gain the victory.

The French nobles appeared to disregard the lessons they might have gained from their loss at **Crecy** (see no. 30). The French army moved forward in confusion, with the nobles competing with each other to see who could ride faster and attack the English sooner. Yet the French crossbow men found their weapons useless because of the heavy tree line that surrounded the English area. When the French came forward on the narrowest part of the road, their greater numbers gained them no advantage. At a signal from Henry V, his army, longbow men and knights charged forth upon the French. There was a terrific slaughter. The English took many knights captive to hold for ransom, but at least 8,000 French lost their lives; among them were D'Albret, three dukes, 90 nobles and 1,560 knights. The English suffered a loss of 400 killed, including the Duke of York.

Following the battle, King Henry V resumed his march to Calais. He had shattered the French nobles in the battle, so he found little resistance. In 1420 he married the daughter of the King of France. Henry died in 1422 anticipating that his young son would soon become king of both countries.

By 1429, the English held Paris, Rheims and the northern half of France, while the uncrowned Dauphin of France, **Charles VII (1403-1461)**, remained in temporary quarters in Chinon, exiled from his true place as king. The situation worsened when the English besieged the key city of **Orleans**, on the Loire River. This was one of the last strongholds belonging to the followers of Charles VII. If it fell, it would appear as if nothing could prevent the English from taking over the entirety of France. At this critical point, a peasant girl from Domremy, in the eastern part of France, appeared to alter the scenario and instil hope to the French soldiers.

Joan of Arc (1412-1431) was an innkeeper's daughter. She began to see visions and hear the voices of three saints (**St. Catherine, St. Margaret** and **St. Michael**) by the time she was fourteen. These voices told her she was to be the savior of the Valois monarchy and of France. She was to go to Chinon and persuade the Dauphin to give her an army, with which she was to raise the siege of Orleans. Not surprisingly, Joan responded that she was a peasant girl; how could she succeed when the knights of France had failed?

In the spring of 1429, she went to Chinon. She must have impressed the Dauphin for he had her examined by a group of priests who pronounced she was of sound mind. He then gave her nominal command of 4,000 men.

Joan and her troops managed to enter the city without having to fight. Once they were within the walls, she sent messages to the English commander, the **Earl of Salisbury**. She warned him not to thwart the will of God, to depart from Orleans and from France itself. The English rejected her overture, and the battle soon began.

On May 3, Joan sent her men forth. They captured the English fort at **St. Loup**. Then they crossed the river and fought on the south

Joan of Arc

side of the Loire river, attacking the English fortifications there. During the fighting, Joan was wounded by an arrow in her shoulder. She had the wound bandaged and then returned to the battle, which aroused great concern among the English. It was at this time that the English developed the notion that she was a sorceress and a witch. The English forts were captured, and the English withdrew from their remaining positions on May 8, 1429.

Within two months of the end of the siege, Joan had accomplished her greatest feat. She led the Dauphin through hostile territory to the great cathedral at **Rheims** where he was crowned on July 17, 1429.

Constantinople (present-day Istanbul), the capital and nerve center of the **Byzantine Empire**, had held out against some 16 sieges over the centuries. Its high walls and natural protection of water on three sides kept it safe against attacks by Arabs, Seljuk Turks, Avars, Huns and numerous other peoples. In 1453, the city was endangerd by the appearance of a new Turkish people, bringing with them a new weapon.

two centuries.

The defense of Constantinople was headed by Byzantine Emperor **Constantine IX**. Only 10,000 people volunteered to fight, so he had a small force with which to withstand an attack of 50,000 men, 56 small guns and 14 heavy cannons. The Ottoman artillery soon began to reduce the walls of Constantinople that had repelled invaders for centuries. The morale of the defenders was very low; the Byzantines had asked for help from their Latin cousins in Rome and the West, but little assistance had come. It seemed as if Constantinople, which had been the bulwark that had protected Europe for centuries, was being left to its fate.

Mohammed II enters Constantinople

By late May, the walls had been shot through and the Turks were ready to make their assault. **Sultan Mohammed II (1430?-1481)** led his men in a charge that brought them into the city. Once inside the walls, the Turks found little

The **Ottoman Turks** had appeared in **Asia Minor** around 1300. They had built up forces and captured most of the Byzantine land on the peninsula by 1400, but had then been set back by an attack on them by the Mongols led by **Tamerlane (1336-1405)** in 1402. The Ottoman Turks came forward to besiege Constantinople in 1453. They brought numerous cannons with them; the Ottomans led the development of artillery for the next

resistance. Emperor Constantine was killed on the steps of a church, and a garrison of 8,900 men were either killed or sold into slavery. The Turks sacked the city for three days, killing some 4,000 inhabitants, relenting only because the Sultan wanted Constantinople as the capital of his own empire. That soon came to pass--the city that stood at the cross-roads of Europe and the Middle East became the pride of the new Ottoman empire.

England fell into a state of political confusion during the so-called **Wars of the Roses**, from 1455 to 1487. The contest was between the **House of Lancaster** and the **House of York**, both of which claimed the right to the throne of England. This baronial conflict involved the population of England since it was difficult to carry out the normal essentials of politics (tax collection, acts of Parliament, etc.) during such turmoil.

Richard III (1452-1485) officially wore the crown. His most active rival was **Henry Tudor VII, the Duke of Richmond (1457-1509)**, the Lancastrian claimant to the throne. A clever manipulator of both men and public opinion, Henry Tudor brought 10,000 men to **Bosworth Field** in Leiceistshire. Richard III met him there with a force of 12,000 men and a small number of field guns.

Richard III drew up the Yorkist army in its typical formation. There was a screen of archers in front, with the main body of infantry behind them, and cavalry on both wings. Henry Tudor's troops were composed mainly of cavalry, although he too put forth a thin screen of archers. It appeared that Richard III was in favor, but to the north of both armies lay a significant body of troops under the command of **Lord William Stanley**, who had publicly made no commitment to either side (in private, he had given his support to Henry Tudor).

The battle began with an exchange of arrow flights. The main body of troops from both armies then closed in and engaged at close quarters. It was typical warfare for late medieval Europe; a combination of sword and pike, armor and leather. At a critical moment in the fighting, Lord Stanley brought his men in to support those of Henry Tudor. Seeing how desperate his cause had become, Richard III charged directly at Henry Tudor, and was killed. With his death, his supporters soon dispersed. Richard's crown was picked out of a bush where it had fallen and placed on Henry Tudor's head.

Bosworth Field ended the Wars of the Roses. It began the Tudor dynasty which would lead England away from the Catholic Church, make England an international power through the seafaring activities of **Sir Francis Drake**, and defeat the **Spanish Armada** in 1588 (see no. 43).

Death of Richard III and coronation of Richmond

Few peoples in the history of the world have fought as relentlessly and over such a long period of time as did the Spanish in their attempt to reconquer the Iberian peninsula from the Arabs and Moors. The **Spanish Reconquista** lasted from 800 AD until 1492 when the key Moorish stronghold of **Granada** fell to the combined armies of King **Ferdinand (1452-1516)** of Aragon and Queen **Isabella (1451-1504)** of Castile.

The two Christian monarchs married in 1469, bringing their two previously separate kingdoms together. During the 1480s they made war upon the Moorish kingdom of Granada, lodged in the very southern part of Spain. Following their capture of **Malaga** in 1487, all that remained to the Moors was the fortress-city of Granada itself, commanded by the last of the Moorish leaders **Abu Abd Allah Mohammed XI (died 1527)**, better known as **Boabdil**, king of Granada.

Though he knew his position was desperate, Boabdil refused to pay tribute to the Christian leaders. In April 1491, King Ferdinand appeared before the city with 80,000 men. Despite the great strength of the city's defenses (augmented by the two castles of the **Albaycin and Alhambra**), the Moors were doomed to starvation or to defeat on the open plain. To show their strength and the irresistible nature of their force, Ferdinand and Isabella built an entirely new city named Santa Fe, six miles west of Granada.

Faced with these difficulties, Boabdil began to negotiate. The surrender took place on January 2, 1492, when Boabdil handed the keys of the city to Ferdinand and Isabella. The Reconquista was finally completed, a long time after the first Arabs and Moors had crossed the **Strait of Gibraltar** in 711 AD.

As a byproduct of their victory, Ferdinand and Isabella felt wealthy enough to sponsor **Christopher Columbus (1451-1506)** on his attempt to find land by sailing west across the Atlantic. Christians everywhere in Europe were as thrilled with the news of the taking of Granada, as they had been downcast over the surrender of **Constantinople** (see no. 33). A number of reckless Spanish warriors, born and raised on the idea of the Reconquista, would, as a result of this victory, turn their energies to the New World.

The Alhambra

In the days of European conquest of indigenous peoples, few victories seemed as thorough and complete as that of **Hernando Cortez (1485-1547)**, the Spaniard who brought down the Aztec empire in present-day Mexico. Historians have analyzed this remarkable conquest and have yet to fully account for all the factors that went into the Spanish victory.

Battle of Cortez with the Mexicans

Cortez landed on the coast of Mexico in 1521. He had only 600 men and a handful of horses with him. Knowing very little about the extent of the Aztec empire, but believing it to be rich in gold, he pushed on all the way to **Tenochtitlan**, present-day Mexico City. Cortez arrived in Tenochtitlan on November 8, 1519, and proceeded to terrify the Indians with gunfire, horses, dogs and Spanish steel. He soon abducted the Aztec emperor, **Montezuma II (1466-1520)**, and began to take gold and silver from the inhabitants. For all of his obvious greed and contempt of the Aztecs, Cortez was daring and resourceful in combat. Learning that a contingent of Spaniards had landed on the coast to arrest him, he left a small number of men in the capital and raced to the coast where he defeated, and then won over the men who had come to arrest him. Racing back to Tenochtitlan, he faced a huge uprising by the Aztec people. Cortez and his men forced their way out of the city on June 20, 1520, which became known to the Spanish as their **Noche Triste**, or **Night of Sorrows**. Nearly 1,000 Spaniards lost their lives that night, as did many of their Indian allies.

Making allies with the **Tlaxcalan** and **Totonac** Indians, who hated their Aztec conquerors because the Aztecs demanded human sacrifices as tributes, Cortez returned and besieged the city on May 26, 1521. Montezuma had died in the earlier fighting, and his replacement as Aztec emperor was determined to resist the Spaniards. The Spaniards and their Indian allies fought their way into the city over the course of two and a half months. On August 13, 1521, they launched an all-out assault and captured the inner part of the city. Cortez and his men had triumphed at an enormous cost in human life. Of the 200,000 Aztecs who had populated the city before Cortez had arrived, only one-third survived. The architectural and cultural achievements of the Aztecs were destroyed by the Spanish in the years of consolidation that followed. Tenochtitlan was critical to the future development of Central and South America as the European desire for gold and glory continued to impact the native peoples of the New World.

The heyday of the Mongols had ended with the death of the great conqueror **Tamerlane (1336-1405)**. His great-grandson, **Baber (1483-1530)**, also known as **Babur**, continued the family tradition with his conquest of northern India. Recruiting an army composed of hard-riding horsemen from Central Asia and mercenaries from the Ottoman Turks, Baber moved from Central Asia into northern India. He conquered the **Punjab** in 1525, then crossed the Indus River with 2,000 men. Volunteers and recruits soon joined him and he gathered a force of 15,000 men by the time he reached **Panipat**, 53 miles north of **Delhi**.

There he encountered an Afghan army of 30,000 to 40,000 men led by **Ibrahim Lodi**. Baber prepared to fight a defensive battle. He drew up his outnumbered men behind a line of baggage carts tied together. In gaps that existed in the line of carts, he inserted cannon that had been brought by the Ottoman Turks.

Ibrahim Lodi could see that Baber had built a strong position. Ibrahim maneuvered for several days, trying to find a way through Baber's defenses. Failing to do this, he made a frontal attack on April 20, 1526.

The Afghans made several efforts to break the line of Baber's men, failing each time. The combination of Baber's defense line and the use of artillery completely flustered the Afghans. Baber then switched to the offensive. Catching his foes offguard, he won a complete victory. Around 15,000 of the Afghans, including Ibrahim, were killed, and Baber went on to capture and hold Delhi and Aga. In the process, he founded the **Mongol** dynasty that would rule India until 1761.

Baber, founder of Mongol Dynasty in India

The Ottoman Turks were the most feared warriors of the sixteenth century. Having captured **Constantinople** (see no. 33), they proceeded to move into the Balkans and threaten all of Europe. Not only did the Ottomans possess the fierce **janissary warriors** (permanent soldiers, drafted as children and required to serve in the army for life), and the best artillery train of their time period, but their leader was a skillful and ruthless man named **Suleiman the Magnificent (1496?-1566)**. If ever there was a time when the forces of Islam seemed ready to conquer those of Christian Europe, that time was the early to mid-sixteenth century.

In 1526 Suleiman brought an army of 80,000 men into the Christian kingdom of Hungary. King **Louis II** of Hungary brought 12,000 knights and 13,000 infantry to the battlefield at **Mohacs**, a town on the Danube. There was some irony in the Hungarians fighting the Ottoman Turks. Both people had originally come from Central Asia (the Hungarians had been the Magyar people who had invaded Europe around 900 AD and became Christianized around 1000). Now the Hungarians were fighting on the eastern fringe of Europe, seeking to fend off the attack by yet another group of people from Central Asia.

The battle was a classic test of cavalry versus infantry forces. The Hungarians made a promising start to the battle, routing several sections of the Ottoman army as they made contact. King Louis and his top nobles led some successful cavalry charges. When the Hungarian horsemen ran into batteries of Ottoman cannon, they suffered heavy losses. Suleiman then launched a counterattack with his best troops, the janissaries and **spahis** (the permanent cavalry equivalent of the janissaries). With the attack of these soldiers, the Hungarians began to disperse and flee. Although many of the Hungarian infantry managed to escape, the great majority of their horsemen were killed on the field. The carnage was such that it took Suleiman three days to reorganize his men in the aftermath of the battle. The Hungarians lost 15,000 men, including King Louis II, seven bishops and over 500 of the top nobles of their country. Suleiman's losses were not counted, but are estimated to have been equally as large. Mohacs gave Suleiman and his successors full control of the Balkan areas. Eastern Europe would remain separate from Western Europe, both politically and culturally, for the next 300 years.

Suleiman the Magnificent

Suleiman besieging Vienna

In the wake of his great success at **Mohacs** (see no. 38), **Suleiman the Magnificent (1496?-1566)**, sultan of the Ottoman empire, decided to press further into Europe. In the late summer of 1529, he advanced from Constantinople with 80,000 men, a large train of artillery, and a fleet of ships to provision his army. His goal has not been determined with certainty. There is good reason to suspect he wanted to defeat **Charles V (1500-1558)**, leader of the Holy Roman empire, whom he viewed as his only significant contender for mastery in eastern Europe.

Suleiman's army laid siege to **Vienna** on September 26, 1529. The sultan sent messages, demanding that Emperor Charles appear to defend the city (the Emperor was in Spain). The defense was led by Marshal **William von Roggendorf**, who had between 17,000 and 20,000 men available for the defense of Vienna. Given the Ottoman's successful record in sieges and the use of artillery, it appeared as if the Turks would prevail.

The northern side of Vienna was protected by the Danube River and the eastern side was guarded by the Weiner Bach River. Suleiman drew up his forces on the south and southwestern sections of the city and placed his cannon there. He soon found, however, that the defenders of Vienna would not yield easily; in fact they conducted a most energetic defense. Von Roggendorf's men had pulled down buildings to give a clear line of fire to their artillery, and also dug trenches to snag the Turkish advance. When the enemy came closer, they conducted a furious counter-bombardment and sent out small groups of men to attack the Turkish lines. Von Roggendorf's supply of men was limited, but their spirit was high.

Suleiman gave up the siege on October 16, 1529. The heavy autumn rains made his return to Constantinople difficult, and the fleet that carried the Ottoman artillery was attacked as it passed by the Christian fortress of Pressburg. It is uncertain how many men Suleiman lost, but some historians have placed the figure as high as 20,000.

Holding Vienna was crucial to the morale of Christian Europe. Although there would be many battles fought in the future with the Ottoman Turks (see no. 41 and no. 42), the single greatest threat to the heartland of Europe was stopped by the vigorous defense of Vienna.

Francisco Pizarro (1470-1541) came from Estremadura, the same section of Spain as **Hernando Cortez (1485-1547)**. Like Cortez, Pizarro wanted to explore new lands and win gold, glory, and honor for himself and his country.

In 1531, Pizarro landed in Peru, on the west coast of what is now called South (or Latin) America. Pizarro soon encountered the subjects and vassals of the **Inca empire**, a land that stretched nearly 2,000 miles in a north-south direction. The Peruvians were ruled by an absolute monarch, the **Inca**, and were not accustomed to outside influence, as geography had isolated them from their neighbors in South America. Therefore, the appearance of 160 Spaniards under a resolute, ruthless and decisive leader threw the northern part of the Inca empire into some confusion.

The Peruvians had just undergone a power struggle between two brothers (**Atahualpa** and **Huascar**) who had fought to see who would become the Inca, or the monarch. Atahualpa prevailed in the fighting in early 1532 and brought his forces to **Cajamarca** on a plateau on the eastern slope of the Andes Mountains.

Such was the audacity of Pizarro and his small band, that they marched from the coast of Peru into the interior, seeking to encounter the Inca and his army. Pizarro led his men over the Sierra mountains and through deserts. The Peruvian forces could have ambushed and destroyed the oncoming Spaniards numerous times, but Atahualpa appeared to have been curious about the foreigners. He allowed them to come into his area, and then withdrew from the city of Cajamarca and camped on the open plain with a force of 30,000 men.

Pizarro was quick to take advantage; he occupied the city and then sent **Hernando de Soto (1500-1542)** (later to become famous as an explorer in North America) to the Inca, inviting him to come into the city as Pizarro's guest. The Inca entered the city late in the day on November 16, 1532, with a bodyguard of 7,000 men. A famous and much-disputed encounter between the Inca and a Dominican friar led to Atahualpa throwing a Bible to the ground and asserting that he himself was a god and did not need the god of the Christians.

Moments later, Pizarro dropped his handkerchief as a signal. A Spanish cannon fired, and the tiny force of Spaniards emerged from buildings and threw themselves at the Peruvians. The sight of the steel Spanish swords, the sound of the artillery, and the ferocity of the attack was too much for the Peruvians. Atahualpa was captured, some 4,000 Peruvians were killed or wounded, and the Spaniards did not suffer the death of a single man. Cajamarca was one of the most lopsided battles in human history. Atahualpa paid Pizarro a large ransom only to be later tried and executed. Pizarro himself later died at the hands of his men in 1541.

Pizarro at Cajamarca

Suleiman the Magnificent (1496?-1566) ruled the Ottoman Empire from 1520 until his death. Frustrated in his siege of **Vienna** (see no. 39), he resolved to root the Christians from their bastion in the heart of the Mediterranean; the island of **Malta**, which was held by the **Knights of Saint John of Jerusalem**.

The knights had a long and distinguished history in the annals of warfare; their origins lay in the

crusading movement 300 years earlier. The Grand Master of the Knights, **Jean de la Vallette**, organized the defense of the island. He had 700 knights, 8,500 men-at-arms and 80 guns with which to withstand the attack of 32,000 Turks, including 6,000 of the much-feared **janissary** troops.

On May 18, 1565, a Turkish fleet of 180 warships arrived at the coast of Malta, led by **Mustapha Pasha** and Admiral **Piale Pasha**. The Maltese harbor was defended by two massive fortresses, **Fort St. Elmo** and **Fort St. Angelo**. The Turks brought their troops to bear against St. Elmo first. Throughout the month of June, Turkish troops attacked in waves of headlong assaults, while Turkish cannon carried out a bombardment of the fortress. When St. Elmo finally fell to the Turks on June 23, the Turkish leaders, accustomed to high casualty lists, were nevertheless appalled at the number of men they had expended to capture one fort. That did not prevent them from turning on Fort St. Angelo, which was guarded by the main Christian force.

Following tremendous cannonades that shook the very rock and foundation of the fort, the Turks made frontal assaults on July 15, August 7, and August 20. Despite the fierceness and skill of their men, the Turks were thrown back each time with heavy losses. Despite their concern over their own casualty lists, Mustapha and Piale knew that the Christians would eventually succumb, if only because of a lack of water. That would have been the case had not a relief army of 10,000 Christians, hastily recruited from Italy and Spain, come to the northern part of the island in September. Soon after, the Turks took to their ships and departed, leaving behind at least 20,000 men killed or wounded.

The defenders had suffered as well. When he went to greet the relief army, La Valette had only 600 men who could still stand and fight. During the course of the siege he had lost 250 knights and 3,000 men at arms killed and 400 knights and 5,000 men at arms wounded.

Despite their defeat at the walls of **Malta** (see no. 41), the **Ottoman Turks** held control of the central Mediterranean during the 1550s and 1560s. They came increasingly into conflict with the ships of Venice, Genoa and Spain, all of whom felt that it would be to their advantage to remove the threat of Ottoman mastery of the inland sea.

The western powers were notoriously envious of one other; Venice and Genoa had fought against each other for centuries. The finale came with **Pope Pius V (1504-1572)**, who formed the **Holy League** in 1571, committing Spain, Venice and the Papacy to fight together against the Turks.

The enormous Turkish fleet of 225 **galleys** and 88,000 men met 233 Christian galleys and **galleases** (a two-decked galley that could carry far more cannon) and a similar force of men in the **Gulf of Patras** (later called **Lepanto**) on the west coast of Greece.

The Turkish right flank of 56 galleys was completely defeated by the Christian left flank of 63 galleys--most of the Turkish ships were run aground and the survivors slain on land. In the center column, the Christian leader, **Don John** of Austria led 63 galleys and a handful of galleases to victory over the Turkish center, comprised of 96 galleys under the leadership of **Ali Pasha**. The cannon fire from the galleases caused great losses to the Turkish archers massed on the decks of their ships.

The area where the Turks had some success was on their left, where 93 Turkish galleys nearly defeated 64 Christian galleys. However, the loss of their right and center so imperiled the Turks that they fled from the battle, giving an undisputed victory to the Holy League and to Don John of Austria.

The casualties were immense. The Christians lost 15,000 men killed, wounded or drowned and 12 galleys sunk. The Turks suffered the loss of 30,000 men killed, 8,000 taken prisoner, 113 galleys wrecked and sunk and 117 captured. It was one of the most complete naval victories ever won, and it gave firm control of the central and western Mediterranean to the Christian powers of Spain, Venice and the Papacy. One modern historian, John Keegan, proposed that the battle has been misjudged; that it was not the loss of the ships that so hurt the Ottoman empire, but the loss of thousands of skilled archers-losses that could not be made up in one generation. Whether one accepts Keegan's view or follows the more traditional interpretation that the loss of ships was crucial, there is no doubt that Lepanto was decisive in halting what might have been a Turkish takeover of Christian Europe.

The Battle of Lepanto

In 1588, King **Philip II (1527-1598)** of Spain attempted to conquer England. He wanted to defeat his arch-rival, Queen **Elizabeth I (1533-1603)** of England, and to bring her country back to what he believed was the one true faith, Catholicism. Philip was a diligent bureaucrat by nature, and he was very involved in the organization of his navy, the **Armada**. Eventually, a fleet of 130 ships collected at the port of **Cadiz**, carrying 30,000 Spanish soldiers and an equal number of sailors. All were given the rites of absolution before they embarked on what they believed was a holy crusade to free England from the curse of Protestantism.

The bulky fleet sailed from Cadiz, but had to put in at Corunna in northern Spain for water and supplies. By the time the Armada approached the southern coast of England, the English were well aware of its presence. The English fleet was commanded by **Lord Howard** of Effingham, but the heart and soul of its leadership was **Sir Francis Drake (1540-1596)**, the intrepid sailor who had disrupted Spanish gold fleets from the New World. Indeed, Drake's raids upon the Spanish had much to do with bringing on the war between England and Spain.

The English fleet of 197 ships sailed out of Portsmouth and challenged the Spanish fleet as it entered English waters on July 21. Although the English ships were faster to maneuver, the Spanish ships carried more guns and were formed up in a crescent for battle. As long as the Spanish remained in that formation, the English could not stop

Landing of English at Calais

their advance; they could only pick off a ship or two from the wings. Through a combination of maneuvering and skill at gunnery, the English sunk ships one by one. By the third day it became apparent that the Spanish could not force a landing in southern England. They headed up the English Channel toward **Calais**, where they intended to rendezvous with another Spanish army, led by the **Duke of Parma**.

The Armada reached the port of Calais, somewhat battered. The Spanish had lost nearly 10 ships to English fire and the morale of some of the captains had fallen. The Spanish commander, **Medina Sedonia**, was a courageous man, but no sailor. He anchored in the port of Calais and sent messages to the Duke of Parma asking for help.

The English then sent fire ships into the port of Calais on the night of July 29. The Spanish managed to fend off the fire ships, but they lost their crescent formation and many captains cut their anchors in order to escape. When morning came, the Armada was dispersed into small groups of ships in the English Channel. The English set upon them and a day of heavy fighting ensued. The Spanish fought with determination, but they ran out of ammunition by late afternoon. The Spaniards decided to escape from the English by sailing north, around Scotland and Ireland, to reach Spain. At least half of the Spanish ships were lost to storms and rocks, and thousands of Spaniards died on the long voyage home.

In spite of the defeat of its **Armada** (see no. 43) on the sea, Spain remained a supreme military force on land for many years. The Spanish **tercios** (infantry units of pikemen drawn up in squares) thwarted its opponents during the early seventeenth century. It was not until the **Battle of Rocroi**, near the Franco-Belgian border, that another European army managed to thoroughly best the tercios and end the era of Spanish domination.

By 1643, the **Thirty Years' War** (1618-1648) had evolved into a slugging match between France and Spain. In that year, 26,000 Spanish troops led by **Don Francisco de Melo** besieged the town of Rocroi. Some 22,000 French troops, led by **Louis II, Duke of Conde (1621-1686)**, approached the town and sought to raise the siege. Confident in his numbers and the superiority of his fighting men, de Melo pulled back from the siege to meet the approaching French army.

Both armies placed their infantry in the center and cavalry on their wings. Conde led the charge on the French right flank, which routed the Spanish horsemen in front of him. On Conde's left flank, the reverse occurred, with the Spanish pushing the French back. At this point, Conde wheeled his cavalry to his left and made a reckless attack upon the Spanish infantry in the center. This movement separated the Spanish tercios (8,000 men strong) from the Italian, German and Walloon troops in the rear. Coming under heavy attack, the Spanish rearguard gave way and fled, leaving the famed tercios to conduct the battle alone. The Spanish tercios fought like lions for the rest of the day; using their pikes they fended off every attack. This was how Spain had won many desperate battles during the Thirty Years' War, but eventually the numerical difference overcame the Spanish. Late in the day, the tercios collapsed. Rather than surrender, many of the Spanish soldiers died fighting.

Conde entered Rocroi in triumph the next day. The Spanish had lost 8,000 men, with 7,000 captured. The French admitted to a loss of 4,000 men, though this may have been an understatement. Following this battle, France gained momentum in the **Thirty Years' War** and by 1660 replaced Spain as the military power on the European continent.

The Duke of Conde

Naseby was the decisive battle of the **English Civil War** (1642-1645) that pitted King **Charles I (1600-1649)** of England against the forces of the English Parliament. King Charles' followers were known as the **Cavaliers**, while the soldiers of Parliament were called either the **Parliamentarians** or the **Roundheads**, because of their close haircuts.

In the spring of 1645, King Charles brought his army out from Oxford to try to reestablish the royal presence in south central England. Charles' right-hand man was his nephew, **Prince Rupert** of the Rhine, who led the horsemen of the Cavalier army. Rupert was ambitious to meet and defeat the Roundheads in battle, in revenge for his loss to **Oliver Cromwell (1599-1658)** at Marston Moor the year before.

Sir Thomas Fairfax commanded the Roundhead army, while Oliver Cromwell was the leader of the Roundhead cavalry. These two men had created what was called the **New Model Army**, a fighting unit that emphasized rigorous discipline. The Roundheads collided with the advance guard of King Charles' army at **Naseby** in Northamptonshire on June 14, 1645.

Both armies deployed their infantry in the center and placed their strongest cavalry on the right, so Prince Rupert's men were able to charge and scatter their foes, while Cromwell's "ironsides" cavalry quickly defeated the Cavalier horsemen across from them. It appeared as if the battle might disintegrate

The defeat of King Charles at Naseby

into cavalry charges alone.

The infantry of both sides soon came to grips with one another. The fighting was fierce in the center, where the King's guards and his most loyal veterans pressed the Roundheads back. At this point, King Charles could well have won the day by bringing in his reserve and ordering an all-out attack in the center, but he was weakened at that moment by the lack of cavalry on his right. Prince Rupert's men had gone off in pursuit of the Roundheads, and King Charles was disturbed by Rupert's absence from the field. One of the king's supporters, believing mistakenly that the day was lost, started to lead the king away from the battlefield. The Cavaliers never regained the momentum they had briefly held. Cromwell's cavalry swarmed all over the Cavalier infantry in the center. By the end of the day, King Charles' men had lost 6,000 killed, wounded or taken prisoner out of a total force of 9,000. The Roundheads had suffered 1,000 men killed or wounded.

King Charles escaped from the battle, but he never regained his position. He fought on intermittently, and eventually surrendered himself to Parliament. Upon learning of intrigues he was carrying out with foreign princes to reinstate himself, Cromwell conducted a trial, which ended with Charles being beheaded on January 27, 1649. This act of regicide (killing a king) occurred only twice in Europe: the second time was the death of King Louis XVI of France in 1793.

England, Scotland, Ireland and Wales underwent significant changes in their relationships to one another during the seventeenth century. In 1603, King **James VI** of Scotland became King **James I** of England as well. Wales was by this time well under the control of England. The question at issue was Ireland's relationship to her sister island across the narrow Irish Sea.

The answer was provided in the **Battle of the Boyne**, fought between the forces of King **William III (1650-1702)** of England, also known as **William of Orange** and King **James II (1633-1701)** of England (who had recently been deposed by William, his own son-in-law, in the **Glorious Revolution** of 1688). William brought a total of 35,000 men to the battle (English and Irish). They marched south to reach the line of the **Boyne River**, which was held by King James II, supported by the Irish Jacobite leader, the **Earl of Lucan**.

On July 1, 1690, William sent two detachments of troops across the river. One group crossed three miles west of **Drogheda**, while the second group crossed farther upstream. The two contingents soon coordinated their forces and launched an attack on the Irish army. James' men were routed at a cost of 1,000 lives. William's men suffered 500 men killed or wounded.

James II fled to France, where he would spend the rest of his life. William III returned to England to celebrate his victory and confirm his role as King of England and Scotland. The battle, which ensured English domination of Ireland, is still celebrated by the **Orangemen** of Ulster (Northern Ireland), who commemorate their affiliation with William III, who was also stadholder (elected magistrate) of the United provinces of the Netherlands.

James II at the Battle of the Boyne

The **War of the Spanish Succession (1702-1713)** pitted **France**, **Spain**, and **Bavaria** against **England**, the **Netherlands**, and the **Holy Roman empire**. When the fighting began, most observers expected the French to prevail, since the armies of King **Louis XIV** had been predominant on the European continent since the battle of **Rocroi** (see no. 44). Those observers did not anticipate the superb generalship of two men, **John Churchill** (also known as **The Duke of Marlborough**) **(1650-1722)** of England and **Prince Eugene** of Savoy.

In 1704, the French and Bavarian armies threatened to overrun a large section of the Holy Roman Empire. Marshal Count **Camille de Tallard** commanded 56,000 men who were about to enter the empire and threaten the capital city of **Vienna**. Churchill, took it upon himself to march 10,000 British troops and 10,000 Dutch soldiers from the Netherlands to Bavaria, where he linked forces with soldiers of the Holy Roman Empire.

Churchill's march and his union with the Imperial forces led by Prince Eugene of Savoy evened out the manpower on the two sides. The French and Bavarians held a strong defensive position and did not expect to be attacked. The sixteenth century **arquebus** and **pike** had yielded to the seventeenth century **musket**, and Churchill perceived the gain in affixing a short bayonet to the musket, combining fire and steel in one instrument.

The British and Imperial troops left camp at two o'clock in the morning and advanced upon the Franco-Bavarian army. At dawn, Tallard's men were startled out of bed by trumpets and alarm signals. Their position, with their right anchored by the Danube River, appeared strong. Churchill had determined that the French center was weaker than its flanks. He had Prince Eugene attack constantly on the right while he waited for the perfect moment to attack the center. Making matters worse for the French, many of their reserve units were bogged down in the village of **Blenheim**.

Churchill threw the weight of his attack against the French center. A rout ensued, during which the British captured Tallard and five other generals. The Franco-Bavarian army was shattered by the attack. Their losses totaled 20,000 killed or wounded and 14,000 captured. The British-Imperial forces lost 12,000 men killed or wounded.

The battle changed the axis of military strength in Europe. Louis XIV's ambitions were frustrated, and Britain sought a "balance of power" on the continent while pursuing expansion elsewhere. Combined with the capture of **Gibraltar** (see no. 59), Blenheim exemplified British military prowess at the start of the eighteenth century.

The Duke of Marlborough

Poltava was the decisive battle fought in the long **Great Northern War**, between Russia and Sweden (1700-1721). It pitted one of the great military geniuses of the time against one of the most ruthless and determined men ever to occupy the throne of imperial Russia.

King **Charles XII (1682-1718)** of Sweden was a daring and intrepid soldier. He had led his tiny Swedish army to victory against the Poles and Russians several times. His opponent was **Peter the Great (1672-1725)**, Emperor of all the Russias. During that era, Russia lacked a port. Seeing the need to develop ports, a merchant marine and a navy, Peter was determined to fight with Sweden for territory on the **Baltic Sea**.

Peter brought an army of nearly 80,000 men to the battle at **Poltava**, a city on the **Vorsla River** in the **Ukraine**, while the Swedes had 17,000 men. The numerical disadvantage did not daunt Charles XII or his men, as they were accustomed to fighting and winning against such odds. Peter had reconfigured the Russian ranks and made his artillery more formidable. He had studied Charles' past tactics, and knew what to expect of his foe.

Peter the Great

Charles opened the battle by mounting an attack at night. Swedish infantry cut through a line of redoubts (small defensive fortifications) to attack the Russian camp. Charles' plan was daring, and it nearly succeeded. His men passed through the redoubts on their left and center, but the Swedes on the right flank became bogged down in a fight. Charles was incapacitated by a wound and unable to take full control of the battle. By daybreak, Peter had rallied the Russians, and overwhelmed and captured the Swedes attacking on the left. He then mounted an active defense against the other two Swedish columns. By the end of the day, the Swedes were spent, with 7,000 dead and 2,600 captured. Charles himself escaped from the battlefield, and sought refuge with the **Ottoman Turks**.

Poltava marked the appearance of Russia as a first-rate military power in the European world. Along with the reforms introduced to Russian society by Peter the Great, it put Europe on notice that Russia intended to play a major part in the political and military affairs of the eighteenth century. Peter soon obtained his window to the west, the city of **St. Petersburg**, which he converted into a naval base, mercantile port, and new capital for his empire.

49. LOUISBURG
April 30 - June 17, 1745

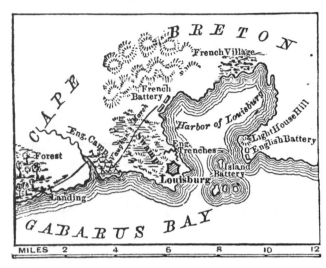

Few military strategists thought of British North America until 1745. When they did, they probably entertained a low opinion of the **Yankee** fishermen and farmers who lived there. Much of that perception would change with the siege of **Louisbourg**, on Cape Breton Island, in **Nova Scotia**.

King George's War, fought between Great Britain and France, began in 1744. Learning of the declaration of war, the governor of the French fort of Louisbourg had his men take and hold the Yankee fishing village of **Canso** in Nova Scotia. In retaliation, the government of the colony of **Massachusetts Bay** decided to strike back against the French. Rather than merely retake Canso, the British-Americans decided to attack and capture Louisbourg itself, a fortress that had been built over twenty years time by expert French engineers. Governor **William Shirley** collected 4,500 British-American militiamen; leadership of the campaign was entrusted to **William Pepperrell** (1686-1759), a fishing and lumber merchant from Kittery, Maine (then part of the Massachusetts Bay colony).

Pepperrell sailed from Boston in March, retook Canso, and proceeded to anchor off Louisbourg. The French defenders were so surprised to see a Yankee fleet and army that they allowed the British-Americans to disembark without impediment. Once ashore, the Yankees found the terrain to their liking. Built to resist an attack by sea, Louisbourg lay in a swampy area, with higher ground to its south and west. The Yankees set up their artillery and began to bombard the fort, assisted by a British squadron led by Commodore **Sir Peter Warren**.

While Warren's ships prevented any supplies or reinforcements from reaching the area, Pepperrell's men brought their guns closer and closer to the city walls. By the time the French agreed to negotiate, the British-Americans had fired thousands of cannon balls into the city. The French hauled down their flag and the Yankees entered the city on June 17, 1745. London rejoiced at the news, and Pepperrell was made a **baronet**, the first hereditary knighthood granted to a North American colonist.

The British-American conquest was followed by a difficult period of occupation. The American soldiers and British sailors bickered over booty from the captured city, and over 1,000 British-Americans died from smallpox the next year. When Britain and France came to terms in the **Treaty of Aix-la-Chapelle** in 1748, Louisbourg was returned to France in return for the restoration of Madras in India. New Englanders were outraged; some historians have attributed the American response to the loss of Louisbourg as one of the first events that started Americans down the long road to independence.

In 1745, the **Stuart dynasty** made its last effort to regain its position in England and Scotland. **James II** had lost his throne to his son-in-law, **William of Orange** in 1688 (see no. 46). James' son, **James Edward Stuart**, was known as the **Old Pretender** to the throne of England and his son, **Charles Edward Stuart (1720-1788)**, was known as the **Young Pretender** or **Bonnie Prince Charlie**.

In 1745, while the **War of the Austrian Succession** raged between England and Austria on one side and France and Prussia on the other, Bonnie Prince Charlie landed a small number of men on the coast of Scotland and declared that he was the lawful ruler of that land. Many of the highland clans rallied to him, as did members of the **Kirk**, the Scottish Presbyterian leadership. In doing so, they took a great risk, for King **George II** of England (known to the Jacobites as **Georgie Pordgie**) was determined to put down all rebellions within his lands.

King George sent his son, **William Augustus, Duke of Cumberland (1721-1765)**, north with 10,000 men to squelch the Stuart supporters. Faced by the English approach, Bonnie Prince Charlie turned north. He and his men thought to outmaneuver their foes by a night march, but when they arrived at **Culloden Moor**, they found that Cumberland and his men were ready and waiting for them.

Cumberland had placed his artillery in such a manner that they could sweep the field with cannon shot. As the Scots (5,000 in number) came under fire, they began to break ranks, attacking the English in an attempt to end the cannonade, as Cumberland had hoped.

The open lines of Scots attacking across the moor were cut to pieces by the artillery and musket fire of the English. As the Scots began to lose heart and withdraw, Cumberland sent in the English cavalry, which showed little mercy. The Scots suffered 1,000 killed and 1,000 captured, while the English losses amounted to 300 men killed or wounded. Bonnie Prince Charlie escaped northward and was helped to France by a young Scottish girl, **Flora Macdonald**. Charles Edward Stuart who died in France, without any children, ending the Stuart dynastic line. For his part, the Duke of Cumberland became known as **Butcher Cumberland** for his remorseless pursuit of the enemy. By a curious coincidence, both sides left a legacy in the New World. Many Scots emigrated to North America in the wake of Culloden, and Flora Macdonald herself played a brief part in the American Revolution. Butcher Cumberland was made immortal in American topography: the famous **Cumberland Gap** from Virginia to Kentucky was named for him by the explorer Dr. Thomas Walker in 1750.

**Charles Edward Stuart,
the Young Pretender**

The subcontinent of **India** had been fought over many times by Muslims, Hindus, Aryans and Mongols, but the appearance of Europeans in the eighteenth century brought a new era to Indian affairs. The newcomers, mainly French and English traders and merchants, brought new types of firepower and sophisticated trading practices intended to make India part of the overseas European empires. An uneasy balance between French and British interests existed until 1756 when the **Seven Years' War** broke out between England and Prussia on one side, and France, Austria, and Russia on the other.

The tiny army of the **British East India Company** pursued that of **Siraj-ud-Daula**, the **Nawab of Bengal**. The Nawab had sided with the French in 1756, and his army had committed atrocities against the English in **Calcutta**. In 1757, the Nawab was pursued by Colonel **Robert Clive (1725-1774)**, who had 800 British troops and 2,200 Indian allies with eight artillery pieces. The Nawab's forces came to 35,000 infantry and 15,000 cavalry.

The disparity of numbers was large but Clive was confident. He discovered that several divisional commanders were plotting against the Nawab. When the large army of the Nawab attacked the British, Clive held his position and fended off the attack, assisted in this by the regulated and disciplined firing of his British troops. The morning attack was followed by a monsoon thunderstorm at midday, during which Clive's men covered their powder and the flints of their flintlock muskets (the Nawab's soldiers failed to take this precaution). After the weather cleared, Clive ordered a series of attacks in the afternoon. Beset by the rapid and accurate fire of the British, the Nawab's army began to disintegrate. By five o'clock Clive had won a complete victory. The British and their allies suffered 72 men killed or wounded, while the forces of the Nawab lost 500 men killed or wounded. The battle gave a clear predominance in India to the British forces, which they would hold until the end of **World War II**.

Robert Clive

Frederick II "The Great" (1712-1786) of Prussia stands tall in the category of remarkable military leaders. Raised in an ultra-conservative and ultra-military family (the **Hohenzollern dynasty** of Prussia), he studied music, art, and poetry in his youth, leading many Europeans to believe he'd be an easy mark when he ascended to the throne.

The **Seven Years' War** (1756-1763), pitting Frederick's Prussia against France, Austria, Russia, Sweden, and Saxony. Prussia's only ally was Great Britain, which under the leadership of **William Pitt (1708-1778)**, devoted its energies toward winning the war on the high seas. Except for some financial assistance from Britain, Frederick was on his own against five powerful foes.

In the fall of 1757, Frederick raced from battle to battle to ward off attacks against the heart of Prussia. Austrian raiding forces entered **Berlin** on October 16, but Frederick kept his eye on the main threat: the combined Austro-French armies led by **Prince Joseph** of Saxe-Hildburghausen and **Prince Charles de Soubise**. He enticed his enemies to converge on the village of **Rossbach** on November 5.

The Austro-French army numbered 64,000 men; Frederick had only 21,000 infantry and 38 squadrons of cavalry. Seeing that the Austro-French leaders intended to envelop his left flank, Frederick pretended to withdraw his infantry to the east, away from the village. The Prussian cavalry, led by General **Friederick Wilhelm von Seydlitz**, also swung wide to the east, while the infantry, once out of the enemy's sight, changed direction and headed south. When the Austro-French forces completed their flanking maneuver, they were greeted by heavy artillery fire, a Prussian cavalry attack on their right flank, and a surprise infantry attack on their left. After less than an hour and a half of combat, the Austro-Franco forces were routed, leaving behind 3,000

Seydlitz at the Battle of Rossbach

killed or wounded, 5,000 prisoners and 67 guns captured. Frederick had lost only 548 men killed or wounded.

Frederick immediately marched to **Silesia** to ward off more attacks and met another Austrian army (65,000 strong) led by Prince Charles at the village of **Leuthen**, in present-day Poland. Commanding 33,000 men, Frederick took the offensive, attacking the Austrians. Moving toward the Austrian right, he then changed direction and attacked the left flank while his cavalry made an attack on the Austrian rear. An **echelon attack** (waves of infantry, attacking in succession) threw the Austrians into confusion, and the Prussian cavalry soon won the day. The Austrians lost 6,750 killed or wounded and 12,000 captured. The Prussians suffered 6,400 men killed or wounded. Frederick captured **Breslau** five days later, taking another 17,000 Austrians prisoner. Frederick's victories demonstrated the fact that mobile armies could defeat larger ones through the use of cavalry and infantry maneuver.

England and France vied for control of the North American continent during the **Seven Years' War** (1756-1763), known in America as the **French and Indian War**. By early 1759, the British had come close to their goal of taking French Canada, but important strongholds remained, most notably, **Quebec City**.

British General **James Wolfe (1727-1759)** brought 9,000 British soldiers on ships up the St. Lawrence river in 1759. He arrived in the Basin of Quebec in June, and found that his opponent, the **Marquis de Montcalm**, had thoroughly fortified the approaches to the city. Montcalm had 16,000 men under arms, although only 4,000 of them were regular troops; the rest were French-Canadian militiamen.

Wolfe landed his men at Point Levy and on the Isle d'Orleans. He made an abortive attack against the French encamped at **Montmorency Falls** on July 31 and lost 450 men. During August Wolfe fell into despair, as he could find no weakness in the French defenses. By early September, he learned of a cove two miles south of the city, and of a steep ascent that led to the **Plains of Abraham**, directly outside the city's walls. Since Montcalm had the majority of his men arrayed on the northern side of the city, Wolfe decided to take a risk.

Under cover of darkness, Wolfe brought 4,500 men by boat to the cove of **Anse de Foulon**. An advance guard of British troops ascended the heights and overpowered the small guard force at the top. No alarm was given, and by dawn Wolfe had nearly all of his 4,500 men on the Plains of Abraham.

When he learned of the British maneuver, Montcalm decided to attack. He marshaled an equal number of men and marched directly into battle at ten o'clock in the morning. The French-Canadian militiamen and their Indian allies threw themselves to the ground and fired at the English, while the French regular troops advanced in a line-of-battle (a tactic of sporadic firing while advancing). The British held their fire until the French had come within forty yards, and then released a deadly stream of musket fire. The French soon broke and ran, suffering heavy losses as they retreated. Wolfe was hit by three musket balls and died on the field, knowing that his plan of battle had succeeded. The Marquis de Montcalm was wounded and died in Quebec one day later. On September 18, 1759, the garrison of Quebec City hauled down the **fleur-de-lis** and replaced it with the **Union Jack** of Great Britain.

The capture of Quebec determined that Canada would fall into the hands of the British. Nevertheless, the French population maintained its language, culture, and customs, and today there is still a strong separatist movement (the **Parti Quebecois**) within the Province of Quebec in Canada.

The death of General Wolfe

While England won critical victories such as **Plassey** (see no. 51) and **Quebec** (see no. 53) overseas, France sought to launch a cross-Channel invasion of Scotland that might redeem her losses elsewhere. The problem was that the French fleet was divided in two, as well as blockaded by British ships, in its bases of **Brest** (on the Atlantic) and **Toulon** (in the Mediterranean). The consistent stream of bad news that came to the French court at **Versailles** during 1759 prompted King **Louis XV** to order Marshal **Hubert de Conflans** to take his squadron out from Brest.

Fortunately for France, the British fleet that was blockading Conflans had sustained damages during a tremendous storm. Conflans led his 21 ships of the line out from Brest on November 14. Unfortunately for France, British Admiral **Edward Hawke (1705-1781)** had set sail that same day with 23 ships of the line and 4 auxiliary 50-gun ships (a typical ship of the line carried from 74 to 98 cannons).

Hawke soon sighted Conflans' ships and gave pursuit. Conflans turned his slightly outnumbered fleet into **Quiberon Bay**, on the east coast of France, which had a notorious reputation for rocks, shoals, and reefs. Hawke daringly followed after them, although he had no local pilots to guide his way.

The battle was fought on a cold, stormy afternoon, within sight of the coast of France. The engagement opened disastrously for the French. They fought with great courage, but the effectiveness of the British gunners and Hawke's larger fleet, turned the battle into a rout. Within a matter of hours, seven French ships had been captured or sunk. One French ship sunk itself by opening its lowest level of

Louis XV

gun ports. Seven others escaped up the mouth of a river, but were rendered ineffective for months to come. The remainder of Conflans' ships made it to port in **Rochefort**. By contrast, Hawke lost only two ships to reefs, and none to the gunnery of his enemy.

Quiberon Bay decisively demonstrated the superiority of the English sailors and gunners. The battle shattered any hope the French had for invading Scotland and ensured that 1759 would be known in England as the "Year of Miracles", when British arms triumphed on both land and sea around the globe.

The first two battles of the **American Revolutionary War** were fought between professional soldiers on one side and farmer-soldiers on the other. The first shot fired at Lexington was known as "the shot heard 'round the world."

Knowing that the American patriots held large quantities of gunpowder and arms at **Concord**, British General **Thomas Gage (1721-1787)** sent 2,000 British troops from Boston to seize these stores. Lieutenant Colonel **Francis Smith** led the British troops by water to Charlestown and then marched through the night to reach Lexington by daybreak. The famed message runner, **Paul Revere (1735-1818)**, had seen two lights hung in the belfry of the Old North Church that night. Knowing this meant the British were departing by water, Revere (and two other dispatch riders, **William Dawes** and **Samuel Prescott**) rode through the night to alert American patriots along the line of the British march. By the time the British reached Lexington, they were met by 70 or so American patriots, or **minutemen**, who had assembled to halt their advance. British Major **John Pitcairn (1740-1775)** rode forth on his horse and cried out, "Disperse, ye rebels, disperse!" It appeared as if the Americans would do so. They began splitting up into small groups and walking away, though they still held their muskets. Someone, however, fired a shot. No one is certain of the identity of the shooter, or whether he was British or American, **Tory** or **Patriot**. What is known is that the shot initiated a general shooting that left seven Americans killed and a number of others wounded. The Americans dispersed; the British gave three cheers and continued on their march, heading for Concord.

Hearing of that first battle, many American minutemen arrived at Concord, summoned from the towns surrounding that area. When the British arrived, they found most of the supplies had been evacuated. A small number of British troops guarded the eastern side of the **Old North Bridge** over the Concord River. When the Americans (on the western side) saw smoke coming from the British camp fires, they thought the British had set the town on fire. The Americans marched on the bridge and fought a short, battle with the British. The British fell back from the bridge and Lt.Colonel Smith ordered a withdrawal to Charlestown and Boston.

"The first blow for Liberty"

The return march was a nightmare for the British. American minutemen positioned themselves behind trees and stone walls to fire at the colorfully uniformed British soldiers. The British were unable to respond to this type of fighting. By the time the British reached Charlestown and the protection of the British ships in Boston harbor, they had suffered 273 men killed, wounded or missing. The Americans lost 100 men during the course of the day, but they learned effective tactics to defeat the British in open battle.

One of the most famous battles in American history, **Bunker Hill**, is actually misnamed, since the fighting took place on **Breed's Hill** just to the south of Bunker Hill.

During the night of June 16, over 1,000 American militiamen left Cambridge, Massachusetts and marched to the Charlestown peninsula. Setting camp on Breed's Hill, overlooking Boston, they dug earthworks and trenches during the night. When the British sentries in Boston detected them the next morning, they found the Americans well dug in on a hill overlooking Boston; an excellent site for American artillery to bombard the British in the city.

Not wanting to give the Americans more time to fortify themselves, British General **Sir William Howe (1729-1814)** decided on an immediate attack. By two o'clock in the afternoon, Howe had landed 2,200 British troops at the base of the Charlestown peninsula. Howe ordered his men to march up the hill and drive the Americans out of their fortifications. In addition to their muskets, each British soldier carried forty pounds worth of equipment in his knapsack.

In contrast to the well-prepared British, the Americans were disheveled in their appearance, low on gunpowder, and had no access to supplies. They awaited the British advance with grim determination. The American commander, General **William Prescott(1726-1859)**, instructed his men "Don't shoot till you see the whites of their eyes," to conserve gunpowder. When the British were within forty yards of the trenches, the Americans let forth a burst of ferocious and accurate gunfire. Hundreds of British officers and soldiers fell in that first volley, and the rest retreated down the hill.

Howe reformed his men at the bottom of the hill. Despite the severity of his losses, he could not believe the Americans could contin-

The Battle of Bunker Hill

ue to withstand the pressure exerted by his professional troops. He led his men up the hill a second time, only to be met with a second withering blast of musket fire.

Howe was wounded with a musket ball to his arm, but he nevertheless rallied his men and directed them in another desperate advance up the hill. The British would have been shattered with a third blast of gunfire had the Americans not run out of ammunition. The British entered the trenches and fought hand-to-hand, where their use of the bayonet gave them the advantage. The Americans retreated from Breed's Hill and went over Bunker Hill on their way back to Cambridge. The Americans had suffered 400 men killed or wounded; the British had expended 1,054 men killed, wounded or missing.

In December 1776, American General **George Washington (1732-1799)** confided in a letter that unless something changed soon, "the game is pretty well up." Washington had yielded **New York City** to the British, been chased across **New Jersey**, and seen his forces dwindle to 4,000 men by the last month of the year.

There was, however, some hesitation on the part of the British and their **Hessian** (German) allies. British generals **Sir William Howe (1729-1814)** (see no. 56) and **Charles Cornwallis (1738-1805)** went into winter quarters, leaving only 4,000 Hessian troops to keep watch on Washington, who was on the southern side of the Delaware River (the Hessians were on the northern side).

By the last days of December, the American cause was truly desperate. Many of Washington's remaining men were scheduled to leave on the last day of the year, when their enlistment would be up. Given the situation,

Washington decided to use those men while he still could. He planned to cross the Delaware at night and surprise the Hessians on the day after Christmas.

The American crossing of the Delaware has been commemorated in a famous painting by **Jonathan Trumbull**, but the artist did not convey the poor shoes and clothing of most of the American troops. In fact, many observers claimed that once the river had been crossed, they could find their way to **Trenton** by a trail of blood, left from the shoeless feet of many of the Americans.

Washington managed to bring 2,400 of his men to Trenton by dawn of December 26. His opponent, Colonel **Johann Rall** and his 1,400 Hessian troops, were sleeping heavily after a hearty Christmas celebration. The Americans approached the town from two different sides and placed cannon in a manner that would allow them to sweep the streets with their fire. Although Rall and his Hessians rose quickly and fought with courage, the battle was over in less than twenty minutes. By eight in the morning, Washington could clearly see the results of his victory: 22 Hessians killed and 918 captured. The Americans had lost only four men killed and eight others wounded. This lopsided victory gave a renewed energy to the American cause.

George Washington at Trenton

Following **George Washington's** (1732-1799) desperate gamble and success at **Trenton** (see no. 57), the British decided to crush the American rebellion once and for all. British General **John Burgoyne** (1722-1792) developed a master plan; three armies would converge on **Albany**, New York and hold the line of the **Hudson river**. By doing so, the British would cut off New England (which was perceived as the heart and soul of the American rebellion) from the rest of the states.

Burgoyne led 8,000 British and Hessian troops and Indian allies south from **Montreal**. He captured **Fort Ticonderoga** on July 4, 1777, and pushed on to the head of Lake Champlain. Only twenty miles separated him from the Hudson River, but those miles were in a heavily wooded and swampy area, and the Americans felled trees to delay Burgoyne's advance. It took the British twenty days to travel the twenty miles to the Hudson.

The other two British armies were already out of the picture. General **William Howe** (1729-1814) had disregarded his orders to rendezvous with Burgoyne, and marched to capture **Philadelphia** instead. The third army, led by Colonel **Barry St. Leger**, had been stopped by the Americans at **Fort Stanwix** in western New York state.

Unaware of the extent of the dangers that surrounded him, Burgoyne began his march to Albany. He made it only as far as **Freeman's Farm** on the west bank of the Hudson where his 7,000-man army was met by 10,000 Americans, led by General **Horatio Gates** (1728-1806) and General **Benedict Arnold** (1741-1801).

The **Battle of Freeman's Farm** took place on September 19. Burgoyne sent forth a detachment of 1,500 men to probe the American lines. These men were soon sent back by a shower of American musket balls,

coming in particular from Colonel **Daniel Morgan's** (1736-1802) Virginia militiamen. Burgoyne reinforced his column and a general battle ensued. Fighting from the cover of the woods, the Americans inflicted 600 casualties upon the British, while suffering only half that number themselves.

On October 7, 1777, Burgoyne tried again. He sent out another detachment to test the American center. By this time, Gates and Arnold had been reinforced and had nearly 20,000 men in total. The British probe was thrown back quickly, and the Americans went over to the offensive. Gates was satisfied to have thrown back the enemy's advance, but Arnold led men against the key British defenses. Charging a German redoubt on his horse, Arnold was wounded in his leg. Nonetheless, he had inspired the Americans, and by the end of the day the British had lost another 600 men and their best defensive positions.

Burgoyne surrendered at **Saratoga** on October 17, 1777. The loss of an entire British army prompted **France** to enter the war on the side of the Americans, making the conflict worldwide.

Burgoyne at Saratoga

Gibraltar

The rock of **Gibraltar** has been fiercely contested in a number of battles and sieges over the centuries, but the most memorable was that between Spain and Great Britain during the **American Revolutionary War**. Spain entered the war in 1779, with the intention of regaining Gibraltar from England, which had taken possession of it in 1704, during the **War of the Spanish Succession**.

A mere 5,000 British troops held Gibraltar when the war broke out. Those men were able to resist the early attacks made by Spanish infantry, but they needed fresh food and water supplies in order to hold their position. In the winter of 1779-1780, British Admiral **George Rodney** (1718-1792) defeated a Spanish fleet and entered the harbor, bringing supplies and reinforcements to the defending garrison, which rose to number 7,500 men.

As peace negotiations were begun in 1781, Spain became anxious to take the fortress before the war was concluded. In September 1782, the Spanish made a final, massive assault on Gibraltar; ten "floating batteries" of cannon had been constructed with the advice of French engineers. Those batteries entered the harbor and commenced a furious cannonade of the fort. Though the batteries had been estimated to be impregnable to either cannon shot or fire, several of them were set aflame by British cannon balls. The remainder of the batteries were then scuttled, and the Franco-Spanish assault petered out. The Spaniards were so discouraged by the whole affair that a British relief convoy was able to slip into the harbor and resupply the garrison in October 1782.

Spanish **King Charles III** wanted desperately to have Gibraltar, but even his foreign minister, the **Count of Floridablanca**, advised him to sign a peace treaty. "How long, Your Majesty, can one rock disturb the peace of three great empires?" he asked, referring to Spain, Britain and France. The final peace treaty, signed in 1783, gave Minorca and Florida to Spain, while Britain held Gibraltar.

By the spring of 1781, both the British and the Americans were worn out from the trials of the **Revolutionary War**. British General **Charles Cornwallis (1738-1805)** relinquished his attempts to capture North Carolina. Instead he marched to a tobacco village on Chesapeake Bay in Virginia called **Yorktown**, where he believed he could be reinforced and supplied by the British fleet.

American General **George Washington (1732-1799)** still hoped that his veteran soldiers, combined with French troops who had landed at Newport, Rhode Island in 1780, could storm and capture New York City. This was Washington's dream of ending the war, but in July 1781, Washington learned that a French fleet was coming to the American coast from the Caribbean. The fleet of Admiral **Paul de Grasse(1722-1788)** would not sail to New York, but rather to the Chesapeake Bay area. Learning this, Washington and the commander of the French troops in Newport, **Jean Baptiste de Rochambeau (1725-1807)**, decided to abandon their plan of attacking New York City and instead marched their combined forces south to Virginia.

The British did not suspect the Franco-American plan. Washington and Rochambeau marched 10,000 men south from the New York City area to Yorktown where they boxed General Cornwallis in by land. Meanwhile, the fleet of Admiral De Grasse had met and turned away a British fleet outside of Chesapeake Bay. By September 20, 1781, the Franco-American army (16,000 strong) had completely encircled Cornwallis' 7,000 British soldiers.

The French and Americans dug elaborate trenches and earthworks, parallels and redoubts that protected the Franco-American troops and their artillery as they crept ever closer to the British lines. On October 8, French and American troops stormed and captured two British redoubts that were central to the defense of Yorktown (young **Alexander Hamilton (1757-1804)** led the American attack). Knowing the danger he was in, Cornwallis sought desperately to escape. He sent his men forth on a night sortie to break up the American redoubts and spike their cannons. The sortie was a partial success, but the Americans and French soon had their guns firing again.

Cornwallis then yielded to the inevitable. On October 19, 1781, over 7,000 British soldiers and sailors laid down their weapons and surrendered in a ceremony that has been commemorated in a famous painting by **Jonathan Trumbull**. The Revolutionary War was over, and America had won its independence from Great Britain.

The surrender of Cornwallis

The **French Revolution** began in 1789 and built to a crescendo in 1792, the year that King **Louis XVI (1754-1793)** and the royal family were attacked at the **Tuileries Palace** inside of Paris. Although the king and his family were not killed, the kings of **Austria** and **Prussia** vowed to protect their royal relatives and put down the revolution in France before the revolutionary spirit spread to their own countries.

During the late summer and early autumn of 1792, a Prussian army of 34,000 men, led by **Karl Wilhelm**, Duke of Brunswick, advanced across the border into France. The French revolutionaries were intimidated by the news, for the Prussian army had proved itself to be the best in Europe during the **Seven Years' War**. There was every reason to believe the Prussians could defeat the revolution then and there.

A makeshift French army was collected in and around Paris. The greater problem was to find officers with experience, for the previous royal army of France had been almost entirely led by the nobles. French General **Francois Kellerman (1735-1820)** led the army northeast to meet the danger of the Prussian approach.

The two armies collided at **Valmy**, a village located between Chalons-sur-Marne and Ste. Menehould, 100 miles northeast of Paris. The French held a slight numerical advantage with 36,000 men and 40 guns.

Rather than a battle between infantry, the collision at Valmy was an artillery duel. The Prussians opened the cannon fire, confident that the under-trained and inexperienced French troops would break when they heard the sound of grapeshot in the air. The French, whether volunteers or con-scripts, held their places in line and the French guns soon returned fire with a deafening sound of their own. The demonstrable enthusiasm of the French troops so dismayed Karl Wilhelm that the Prussians withdrew by the end of the day; the Prussians lost 180 men killed or wounded, while the French lost 300 men in the cannon fire exchange. Kellerman rightly claimed victory and the Prussians retreated across the border.

Storming of the Tuileries

In the summer of 1798, French General **Napoleon Bonaparte (1769-1821)** set sail from Toulon, headed for Malta and then Egypt. He intended to conquer a section of the Middle East and set up an empire in the tradition of **Alexander the Great (356-323 BC)**.

The French fleet and its transports brought Napoleon safely to **Alexandria**, Egypt. After disembarking from their ships, the French fought and won the **Battle of the Pyramids** that destroyed the power of the Mameluke sultans in Egypt. However, Napoleon had forgotten the long arm of the British Navy and its preeminent admiral, **Horatio Nelson (1758-1805)**.

Nelson failed to catch up with the French fleet prior to the landing of Napoleon's army. He searched relentlessly for the French ships, and in the mid-afternoon of August 1, he came across the fleet of 13 ships of the line and 4 frigates, anchored in Abukir Bay.

French Admiral **Francois-Paul Brueys** was in a well-ensconced position. His ships were anchored tightly together with their best guns and gunners pointed seaward. In creating this type of defensive formation, Brueys was actually copying an earlier British Admiral, **Sir Samuel Hood**. Nelson, who had served under Hood in the Caribbean, knew both the strengths and weaknesses of the French position. He took a great risk by deciding to attack on sight rather than wait until the next morning.

The British ships came straight at the French, but rather than firing at them, a number of the British ships maneuvered and successfully slipped around the French. Within half an hour's time, half of the British fleet was on the leeward (land) side of the French, which was completely unprotected. Brueys had not opened the gun ports on his landward side.

The Battle of the Pyramids

The **Battle of the Nile** was a complete victory for Nelson and a terrible disaster for the morale of the French navy. The French fought with abandon in spite of the hopeless odds, and their casualty lists grew as the evening wore on. Brueys was killed and his flagship, L'Orient, blew up in a tremendous flame when the gunpowder magazine exploded. By midnight, the rout was complete. The British captured or sank 12 French ships of the line that night and 3,000 to 4,000 French sailors were lost to cannon fire, explosions, or drowning.

The battle gave Great Britain complete control of the Mediterranean Sea. Napoleon returned to France in 1799 and never again sought to emulate the Middle Eastern conquerors of two thousand years earlier.

Nelson before the Battle of Trafalgar

Napoleon Bonaparte (1769-1821), master of the European continent, could not find a way to strike against Great Britain. Always the fleet of Admiral **Horatio Nelson (1758-1805)** blocked Napoleon from conquering England. In 1805, Napoleon decided to combine his fleet with that of Spain. If he could gain control of the English Channel, he could bring his army across to England and defeat the only country that had withstood him.

The French admiral, **Pierre de Villeneuve**, was well aware of the fighting qualities of Nelson and the British fleet. It was only in response to repeated orders and jibes from Napoleon that Villeneuve brought the Combined Fleet (36 ships of the line) from the Spanish port of **Cadiz** in September, 1805.

Nelson swiftly brought the British fleet of 33 ships of the line southward, and the two fleets came into eye contact off the coast of Spain. Nelson conferred with his captains the night before the battle. He intended to disregard the normal battle plan which matched two fleets equally, ship for ship, line for line, that almost ensured a draw. Rather, Nelson and his captains would approach the Franco-Spanish fleet in two lines, coming in at right angles to the foe. Once the two fleets came to grips, Nelson believed that "no captain can do wrong who lays his ship alongside that of his enemy." Villeneuve, flustered by Nelson's reputation, had no definite plan of battle, which increased the sense of doom for the combined Franco-Spanish fleet.

On October 21, 1805, after hoisting his famous signal, "England expects every man to do his duty," Nelson led the British lines against the enemy. The Combined Fleet had a precious half hour in which to fire at the oncoming British ships. Many British casualties were sustained in those thirty minutes, but once the British had penetrated the Franco-Spanish line, they gave much more than they had received. British gunners, who had more practice time than their opponents, wreaked havoc on the French and Spanish ships.

Nelson was shot down by a French marksman as he paced the decks of his flagship, Victory. When he was told that at least fifteen ships of the enemy had struck their flags, he retorted that he had expected at least twenty to do so. He died on board the Victory.

Villeneuve was taken prisoner, as were thousands of his men. The total Franco-Spanish casualties totaled 14,000 men killed, wounded or taken prisoner. It was a disastrous day for France, and ended Napoleon's dream of subduing the British Isles.

The defeat of the French fleet at **Trafalgar** (see no. 63) was only one of **Napoleon Bonaparte's (1769-1821)** problems. He had marched eastward to confront a new danger, that of a strong alliance between Russia and Austria that threatened to break up his control of central Europe

On December 2, 1805, Napoleon fought against his foes in what has been called the **Battle of the Three Emperors: Tsar Alexander I of Russia (1777-1821)**, **Emperor Francis II** (1768-1835) of Austria, and Napoleon, who had crowned himself **Emperor of France** in 1804. The allied forces held the advantage in numbers: there were 60,000 Russians and 25,000 Austrians under the command of General **Mikhail Kutuzov**, arrayed against 73,000 French troops. The battle was fought in present-day Slavkov, five miles east of Brno, in Czechoslovakia.

Napoleon was at the height of his power. One of the greatest strategists ever to take the field, he took advantage of fast-moving developments. The battle began when Kutuzov launched an attack on the French right flank. Napoleon reinforced his right and contained the assault. Meanwhile, on his left, Napoleon's men were pushing the allies steadily back to the east. The battle might have ended in an inconclusive draw, but Napoleon seized the initiative and threw his reserve to attack the allied center. The French captured the high ground, and

Kutuzov threw in his own Russian Guard to counterattack. Napoleon put in every man he had available, and the French held the key center position. They advanced to the town of **Austerlitz**, cutting the Russian-Austrian army in two. French cavalry raced to the rear of the enemy and carried out a successful envelopment. The Russians and Austrians caught in the trap fought with desperation but could not break free. Those who tried to escape across the frozen lake drowned as the ice gave way.

Austerlitz became Napoleon's greatest victory. It demonstrated his skill as a battle leader, and the reckless courage of the French

The evening before Austerlitz

armies that he had molded. The French lost 8,500 men killed or wounded; the Russians and Austrians lost 16,000 men killed or wounded and 11,000 taken prisoner. Austria soon sued for peace and the **Third Coalition**-Russia, Austria and Great Britain-that had challenged France was thwarted by Napoleon's victory at Austerlitz.

While she continued to fight against **Napoleon Bonaparte (1769-1821)** on the continent of Europe, Great Britain also went to war with her former colonies, the United States of America. The **War of 1812** dragged on for two and a half years. At first the British were able to do little, since they were also fighting the French, but after the abdication of Napoleon in May, 1814, Britain was able to focus its attention and sent thousands of well-trained veterans to America to intimidate the former colonials for having thwarted Britain during her long contest against Napoleon (Britain and America had feuded over free trade and sailors' rights).

The British captured and burned **Washington D.C.** in August 1814, but were repulsed at Baltimore and again on Lake Champlain. The last British hope for a successful conclusion to the war was to capture the rich merchant city of **New Orleans**. Toward this end, British General Sir **Edward Pakenham (1778-1815)** brought 8,000 British veterans to Lake Borgne and then transported them by boat to the Mississippi River.

Knowing the city was in danger, American Major General **Andrew Jackson (1767-1845)** organized a defense with 5,000 militiamen; volunteers from Kentucky and Tennessee, and a handful of Creole pirates led by **Jean Lafitte**. Jackson placed the city under martial law. The British advance across Lake Borgne caught him by surprise, and by December 20, the British were within just eight miles of New Orleans.

When he learned of this, Jackson exploded, "By the Eternal! They shall not sleep on our soil." Instead of remaining on the defensive, he launched a night attack on the British camp. In the fighting that followed, neither side gained an advantage, but Jackson's energy persuaded the British not to attack the city until they had brought all of their forces together.

Meanwhile, Jackson and his men dug trenches and earthworks between a canal and the Mississippi River itself, blocking the British advance. On this narrow strip of land, the American sharpshooters would have an advantage.

Despite warnings from his subordinates, Pakenham launched a frontal assault on the morning of January 8. Thousands of British troops, carrying ladders to scale the American earthworks, advanced across the field. They

were met by the fire of musket balls and rifle shot. As the morning fog cleared, the American marksmen were able to aim with greater accuracy. Pakenham and his second-in-command were killed in the firing. Within twenty minutes, the British had lost 2,100 men killed, wounded, missing or captured.

The battle confirmed American possession of the mouth of the Mississippi and the key city of New Orleans.

The Battle of New Orleans

Following the **Duke of Wellington's (1769-1852)** many victories over the French in Portugal and Spain, a match-up between him and **Napoleon Bonaparte (1769-1821)** seemed inevitable. The two greatest soldiers in the European world came to battle at **Waterloo** in Belgium.

Napoleon had abdicated his throne in 1814 and been exiled to the island of **Elba** in the Mediterranean. In the spring of 1815, he escaped the island, went to France, and rallied the population against the restored Bourbon monarchy of King **Louis XVIII (1755-1824)**. Napoleon said he was content to have his throne back and that he wanted peace, but the other European powers did not believe him. A coalition of nations formed against him and by June, Napoleon was fighting against the British troops of the Duke of Wellington and the Prussian army of Field Marshal **Prince Blucher**.

Napoleon defeated the Prussians at **Ligny** on June 12 and pushed on toward the city of Brussels. He found Wellington's army of British and Dutch troops dug in on **Mount St. Jean**, which lay directly along the road to Brussels. On the morning of June 18, Napoleon laid out his battle plans to his marshals. He intended a straight-ahead assault after two hours of artillery bombardment to soften up the defenses. One of the marshals informed him of the accurate fire and stubborn defense of the British troops, but Napoleon commenced the battle.

Time and again, the French advanced over broken ground and assailed different sections of Wellington's lines. They made considerable progress on their left flank, but were stalled in the right and center. In the mid-afternoon, French Marshal **Michel Ney** (1769-1815) led a series of daring cavalry charges against the British artillery and infantry squares. Ney lost thousands of horsemen in the attacks. Had

Napoleon then committed his reserve (the famed **Imperial Guard**), they would probably have swept the British off the field.

However, Napoleon spotted a small cloud of dust approaching from the southeast and guessed correctly that it was Blucher's Prussian soldiers advancing, thus he hesitated to commit his last reserve of men. When Napoleon finally did send in the Guardsmen, Wellington had reformed his battle lines. As the Imperial Guard advanced over a crest near the top of Mount St. Jean, the British and Dutch rose from their earthworks and delivered a tremendous set of volleys directly into the ranks of Napoleon's veterans. Men who had won the battles of **Marengo**, **Austerlitz** (see no. 64), **Jena**, **Auerstadt** and **Borodino**, broke and ran when the shots thinned their ranks. At that moment, Wellington stood high in his stirrups and waved his hat; the signal for a general British advance down the hill.

The French army faded into the night, with losses of 25,000 men and 8,000 taken prisoner. The British, with 15,000 killed or wounded, had fought their final battle against Napoleon, who was soon sent to the island of **St. Helena** in the Atlantic Ocean.

Napoleon at Waterloo

There was a struggle for independence from Spain in South America, as fierce and inspired as the **American Revolution** had been. Led by the Colombian patriot **Simon Bolivar (1783-1830)**, thousands of Spanish, Creoles, and Indians in South America carried out revolutions against Spanish rule during the first 25 years of the nineteenth century. The final, climactic battles took place in Peru in 1824.

Simon Bolivar and his trusty lieutenant, **Antonio José de Sucre (1793-1830)**, arrived in Ecuador in July 1822, along with 3,000 veteran soldiers. In 1824 they pursued an army of royalists and Spanish soldiers led by Viceroy **José de la Serna** and General **José Canterac** north from the city of Lima.

They caught up at **Junin**, 95 miles northeast of Lima. Although each army numbered 9,000 men, the battle itself was fought strictly between the two cavalries, about 2,000 men each. Both armies fought with lance and sword, and not a single shot was fired during the battle. The patriots were victorious, and the Spanish soldiers and royalists retreated into the highlands southeast of Lima. Bolivar left Sucre in command of the army and went to Lima to organize a new government.

Sucre pursued the retreating royalists for months. He finally caught up with them at **Ayacucho**, 200 miles southeast of Lima. By then, Sucre had 5,800 men and Serna had close to 9,000 troops. Serna launched an attack against the patriots with both his foot soldiers and his artillery. The left and center of the patriots held firm against the attack and Sucre's right flank, com-

posed mostly of cavalry, swept around the enemy and pushed aside their left flank. At that point, Sucre threw in his reserves and the battle turned into a rout.

Serna was captured as were 14 Spanish generals. He soon signed a capitulation that promised to remove all Spanish troops from Peru, and the republic of Bolivia (named for Simon Bolivar) was established on August 6, 1825. The twin battles of Junin and Ayacucho ended any possibility that Spain could hold onto Latin America; what remained to be seen was what type of governments would be erected in place of the Spanish rule that had lasted nearly 300 years, from the days of Cortez and Pizarro.

Simon Bolivar

The conflicts between Americans, Mexicans, Texans, and Indians in what is now the state of **Texas** began around 1820. When Mexico won her independence from Spain, she encouraged Americans to settle in Texas, under the provision that they would become Mexican citizens and Catholics. As late as 1830 it was not clear which group of people would become dominant in what is now the American southwest. That question was to some extent answered by the battle of **San Jacinto**.

Beginning in 1821, Americans crossed the Sabine river into Mexican-controlled Texas. Setting up farms and homes there, the American-Texans soon numbered 30,000, in comparison to only 4,000 Mexicans in the state. Realizing the danger of the Yankee influx, the president and dictator of Mexico, General **Antonio Lopez de Santa Anna (1795-1876)**, provoked a war with the Texans in 1836. Texas declared its independence from Mexico and established itself as a separate country.

Santa Anna marched north from Mexico with 6,000 soldiers. He stopped to besiege the **Alamo**, an old fortress that was defended by 184 men, including **Davy Crockett (1786-1836)** and other legends of the American frontier. The Mexicans launched numerous frontal attacks on the old fort. When they finally crossed the walls and killed the remaining defenders, the Mexicans found they had lost 1,500 men in the siege. They had also given rise to a new rallying cry for the Texans, "Remember the Alamo!"

A few weeks later, Santa Anna captured 300 Texans at **Goliad.** After their surrender, these men were blindfolded and shot to death. This action provoked another cry, "Remember Goliad!"

The Texans regrouped under the leadership of General **Sam Houston (1793-1863)**. Well

The Battle of the Alamo

aware of the desperate state of the war for Texas, Houston withdrew slowly in the face of the Mexican advance. When he did turn and fight, Houston showed the determination of a lion. He surprised the Mexicans at San Jacinto on April 21, where they were resting after a noonday meal. Over 1,500 Mexicans were defeated by a much smaller Texas force, and Santa Anna became Houston's prisoner.

Santa Anna promised that Texas would be recognized as free and independent, but both he and the Mexican government broke this vow upon his return to Mexico. A cold war would grow along the Texas-Mexican border for the next ten years.

The war between the United States and Mexico (1846-1848) grew out of the Texas question: was Texas still in the hands of Mexico, was it an independent nation, or did it belong to the United States? When the United States annexed Texas in 1845, war with Mexico was inevitable.

The war began favorably for the Americans in April 1846. Although the Mexican army was larger in numbers, it was not as well-schooled as the **West Point** trained U.S. officer corps. The disparity between the two sides in artillery was also considerable. Early American victories failed to persuade Mexico to sue for peace, and therefore American General **Winfield Scott (1786-1866)** was ordered to land at **Vera Cruz** and march to capture **Mexico City** itself.

Scott made a successful landing at Vera Cruz and began to march inland, following much the same route that Hernando Cortez had taken 226 years earlier. The Americans proved adept at living off the land and fending off numerous attacks by the Mexicans. They reached the outskirts of Mexico City on September 1, 1847.

In order to capture the city, Scott had first to subdue the fortress of **Chapultepec**, located on a hill of the same name. Once the summer home of the viceroys of Mexico, since 1833 it had been the Mexican military college, the equivalent of West Point. Colonel **Nicolas Bravo** commanded the garrison of 1,000 men plus the cadets of the college.

Scott had 7,000 men while Santa Anna commanded 16,000 men in and around the city. On the morning of September 12, the

General Winfield Scott

Americans began a furious bombardment of Chapultepec. The firing went on all day, shaking the walls of the citadel and inflicting casualties to the Mexicans within. Colonel Bravo sent messages to Santa Anna, asking for reinforcements, but Santa Anna replied he had none to spare.

At eight o'clock on the morning of September 13, the Americans assaulted the citadel from two sides. General **John Quitman's** troops ran into a column of Mexicans outside the fort, and their battle stopped Quitman from participating in the attack. General **Gideon Pillow's** men went straight at the fortress. They crossed the south wall before the Mexicans could fire their mines, and then fought furiously to gain the inner walls of the fort. Bravo's garrison was so depleted that the Mexicans could not offer a strong resistance. The 51 cadets of the academy fought to the death and became known in Mexican history as the **Ninos Heroes**.

The American flag was planted on Chapultepec, and further actions during the day scattered the Mexican forces in front of the city. Santa Anna lost heart with the fall of Chapultepec. On September 14, he and his troops left Mexico City. Scott and the American army soon occupied the city, the first capital of another nation that Americans had ever entered in force. The battle of Chapultepec ensured that the United States would gain what is now the American southwest (Arizona, New Mexico, Colorado and California) and made the United States a truly "continental" power.

One of the crucial battles of the **American Civil War** (1861-1865) was fought at Sharpsburg, Maryland, between the **Confederate Army of Northern Virginia**, led by **Robert E. Lee (1807-1870)**, and the **Union Army of the Potomac**, led by General **George B. McClellan (1826-1885)**. Lee was a risk-taker, a bold and innovative tactician, while McClellan was a meticulous planner. The two armies and the two different styles of leadership clashed in the early autumn of 1862.

Lee wanted to win a battle on northern soil, to persuade the European powers of Britain and France to recognize the Confederacy. McClellan wanted to eject Lee and his army from the North. The two armies collided on September 17.

Battle at the bridge of Antietam

Lee's 38,000 men were forced to fight on the defensive, which ill-suited their temperament and Lee's style of command. McClellan's 75,000 men held a clear advantage in numbers, but their leader was not accustomed to seizing opportunities quickly.

The Union attacked on its right, and Lee was so hard-pressed on his left that he had to bring many men over from his own right flank to contain the threat. The fighting then spread toward the center of the battlefield, focusing on what came to be called **Bloody Lane**, made bloody by the fierce hand-to-hand fighting between Union and Confederate troops. While this battle raged, Union General **Frederick Burnside** nearly broke through on the Confederate right. His men were in fact poised to attack **Sharpsburg**, but the sudden appearance of a body of Confederate cavalry under General **A.P. Hill** thwarted Burnside and subdued the immediacy of the threat. Only nightfall brought an end to the battle. Lee withdrew under the cover of darkness, and McClellan made no move to stop him. The next day, the Union army remained in camp and did not pursue Lee, to the disappointment of President **Abraham Lincoln (1809-1865)**.

The Confederacy lost 10,318 men while the Union lost 12,401. These figures do not reflect the extent of damage to the Confederate army and morale. Lee simply could not afford these losses, and he had failed to win the battle on northern soil that he needed to demonstrate the viability of the Confederacy to foreign nations.

Abraham Lincoln realized the importance of the Union victory. He was emboldened to publish the **Emancipation Proclamation** on September 23, freeing all slaves who were in areas that had not yet been conquered by the Union army.

Pickett's Charge

During the early summer of 1863, Confederate General **Robert E. Lee (1807-1880)** made one last attempt to win a battle on northern soil. He led the **Army of Northern Virginia** out of quarters and crossed into Maryland and then Pennsylvania, hoping to divert the armies of the North from their attacks on Virginia.

Lee won the battle of **Chancellorsville**, but at great cost. His most reliable general, **Thomas "Stonewall" Jackson (1824-1863)**, had been killed late in the battle. Lee pushed north, and on the morning of July 1, Confederate troops, looking for shoes (they were often poorly supplied), encountered **Union** troops in the town of **Gettysburg,** Pennsylvania.

The Union troops were pushed south through the town, but they rallied as reinforcements arrived. The Northerners took advantage of a great line of natural defense: **Culp's Hill**, **Cemetery Hill**, **Little Round Top** and **Big Round Top**. Using these hills as an anchor to hold their line, the Union forces waited until the main body of their troops arrived under General **George B. Meade**.

Lee had to attack at once, because every hour that passed brought in more reinforcements to the Northern side. On the second day of fighting (July 2) he sent General **James Longstreet's** men forth; they routed a body of Union troops and very nearly turned the Union left flank. Hasty action, desperate fighting, and luck enabled the Union troops from Maine to hold onto Little Round Top, from which Confederate cannon could have swept the entire Union position.

Lee was confident in his men. He believed the Army of Northern Virginia could achieve any objective, but he was lacking one of the crucial elements that had produced past successes: the Confederate cavalry. Over the objections of General Longstreet and others, he planned a frontal assault on the Federal lines at Cemetery Ridge for the afternoon of July 3. A furious Confederate artillery bombardment during the morning and early afternoon made little dent upon the Union lines. When the men of General **George Pickett (1825-1875)** made their charge up the hill, they were met by the rifle shots of thousands of Union defenders.

"Pickett's charge" was the greatest tactical error that Lee ever made. Thousands of Confederate men were killed and wounded in a desperate attack that gained nothing. On the morning of July 4, Lee and his army left the town and headed south. Combined with the fall of the Confederate fortress of **Vicksburg** on July 4, the defeat at Gettysburg spelled doom for the Confederacy, the slave labor-based economy of the South, and the Southern way of life.

SEDAN
September 1, 1870

In 1870, France challenged the growing power of Prussia. Historians and journalists who remembered the Napoleonic wars expected France to win this contest handily, but arms merchants and experts in military affairs predicted a surprise victory by the Prussians.

France was led by **Napoleon III (1808-1873)**, nephew of **Napoleon Bonaparte (1769-1821)**. In the summer of 1870, he was diplomatically outmaneuvered by the Prussian Chancellor **Otto von Bismarck (1815-1898)** into declaring war on Prussia. Napoleon went to the front to command his armies in person.

The French army had plenty of fire and spirit. It also had the **chassepot**, or **bolt action rifle**, which fired more rapidly than any weapon possessed by the Prussians. The Prussian general staff was highly dedicated and organized, and its leaders took advantage of new technologies like railroads and telegraph messages.

Napoleon and General **August Ducrot** marched with the French army of Chalons, seeking to relieve the city of **Metz**, which was under siege by the Prussians. On August 31, the French fell back on **Sedan**, and were surrounded by two converging Prussian armies. There followed a desperate struggle by the French to break out of the trap that Prussian Field Marshal **Helmuth von Moltke** had laid for them. The Prussian superiority in field guns (the steel cannon) was more than a match for the bronze artillery or chassepot of the French. Metz fell to the Prussians.

On September 2, 1870, Napoleon surrendered, along with nearly 70,000 of his men. Prior to the surrender, the French had lost 17,000 men with 21,000 missing. It was the greatest disaster to befall the French army since **Waterloo** (see no. 66), and the loss seriously undermined the confidence of future French leaders in military solutions. Napoleon went into exile. The **Second French Empire** was replaced by the **Third French Republic**, which would last until 1940.

Bismarck at Versailles

73. LITTLE BIG HORN
June 25, 1876

The American Indian wars reached their climax in the two decades after the American Civil War (1861-1865). A handful of daring and resolute Indian chiefs tried to prevent the white man from advancing further west. Though their efforts were fruitless, they left a legacy of pride and dignity that have continued to inspire all Americans.

American Colonel **George Armstrong Custer (1839-1876)** was one of the principal "Indian fighters" of the U.S. Army. Having gained experience during the Civil War, he led troops through **Sioux** Indian territory from 1873 to 1874. The Sioux reserved a special anger for Custer, whom they called "Yellow Hair," because of the atrocities he had carried out against them.

The United States army sought to crush the Sioux uprising in the spring of 1876. General **Alfred H. Terry**, in command of the overall operation, led a large column of men southward while General **George Crook's** men advanced northward into Sioux country. Seeking to converge on the Sioux camps in present-day South Dakota, Terry's men ran into a stumbling block; the pride and egotism of Colonel Custer. Determined to outshine his fellow officers, Custer launched a premature attack on the Indians encamped along the **Little Big Horn River**. Custer and five of his cavalry troops (276 men) ran straight into a Sioux ambush and were swamped by 2,500 Sioux and **Cheyenne** warriors. The Indians had the advantage of numbers and equal weaponry; many of the mounted Indians had **Winchester repeating rifles** that more than neutralized Custer's single-shot carbine pistols. Custer and his five cavalry troops were completely wiped out at a cost of 50 men lost for the Indians.

Custer's Last Stand, as it has been called, was actually a last hurrah for the **North American Plains Indians**. From that time forward, the United States government and army took the threat of Indian raids more seriously and prosecuted the war against the Sioux with greater vigor.

Custer, firing two hand guns, at Little Big Horn

80

The presumption of European superiority took a blow on March 1, 1896, when Ethiopian warriors overwhelmingly defeated an army of Italians and their native allies. The **Battle of Adowa** caused many liberal Europeans to cheer for the setback to imperialism and imperialists to reconsider their relationships with native peoples.

Menelik II (1844-1913) was the ruler of **Shewan** (a southern region of Ethiopia), and since 1889 had been acknowledged as the King of Kings in that country. Though Europeans would refer to him as an Emperor, his true position was that of first among equals of the leaders of Ethiopia. His position, and that of his country, was threatened by the presence of Italian soldiers. Italy had taken land to the southeast of Ethiopia in 1891 and dubbed it **Italian Somali land**. Then Italy took **Eritrea** to the northeast, depriving Ethiopia of its access to the ocean. Finally, late in 1895, Italian troops invaded **Tigray**, an Ethiopian province in the north.

Menelik and **Taytu** (his warrior empress) marched north with roughly 100,000 Ethiopian warriors. At **Amba Algae**, the Ethiopians met 2,500 Italians, who were defending a fort. In six hours of fighting on December 7, 1895, the Ethiopians lost 500 men killed, but won the battle. The Ethiopians besieged another Italian fort at **Mequelle** (January 4 to 19, 1896) which ended with the surrender of the Italian garrison. Menelik allowed the Italians to withdraw from the fort. Despite these two Ethiopian victories, Italian General **Oreste Baraderi** continued to press on, and on February 29, 1896, the 17,700-man Italian army entered the bowl-like area of Adowa, where Menelik was waiting with his large army.

The Ethiopians attacked the following morning at 6:10 a.m. It took four Ethiopian generals and 25,000 men to break the Italian

center, but once that was accomplished, the remainder of the Italians and their allies were put to rout. By 12:30 p.m. the battle was over, and many Ethiopian women (who had accompanied their husbands to war) roamed the battlefield, crying out, "Kill, kill! The brave man will bring me a trophy" (a victim's body part). The Italians lost 6,500 killed or wounded and 2,500 taken prisoner.

The Ethiopian triumph was reported in newspapers around the globe. Crowds in Rome were reportedly heard to chant, "Viva Menelik!" Given the unpopularity of the war at home and the serious losses suffered in the battle, the Italian government began peace negotiations with Ethiopia on March 9, and signed an agreement on October 26, 1896. King **Humbert I** of Italy and the **Emperor of Ethiopia** gave their promise that the two countries would be equal and asserted the "absolute independence of the Ethiopian Empire as a sovereign and independent state." Italy would break its word in 1935 and initiate another Italian-Ethiopian war.

AFRICA
about the middle
of the 19th Century

The battle that brought fame to **Theodore Roosevelt (1858-1919)** and the **Rough Riders** of the **First Volunteer Cavalry** was actually fought on **Kettle Hill**, part of the **San Juan Ridge** overlooking the city of Santiago, Cuba. The battle was the key land fight in the three-month-long **Spanish-American War**.

Lieutenant Colonel Theodore Roosevelt recruited men from the western states as well as Ivy League graduates for his special volunteer regiment, the Rough Riders. Long interested in warfare and in wanting to prove his prowess, Roosevelt added his men to the American invasion of Cuba that began when the Americans disembarked at **Daiquiri** and began their march toward **Santiago**. By the end of June, they had reached the jungle area that lay directly in front of the San Juan mountain ridge, 15 miles west of Santiago. As long as the Spanish could keep control of the ridge, they could block the American advance, but Spanish General **Arsenio Linares** allocated a mere 521 men for the defense of the ridge and the ridge of **El Caney** to the southeast.

The American troops were up at 4:00 a.m. on the morning of July 1, 1898, and **Allyn K. Capron's** battery began firing at the Spanish positions at 6:30 a.m., followed by another artillery barrage at 8:00 a.m.. Given the disparity in numbers and weight of artillery, it seemed certain the Americans could take both Kettle Hill and El Caney, but confusion in battle orders led to hundreds of Americans milling around in the open ground between the jungle and the mountain ridge. The Spanish opened fire with their **mousers** (rifles that used smokeless powder), inflicting many casualties to the Americans, who were still waiting for orders to advance. An American observation balloon was shot down around 11:30 a.m., damaging American morale still further.

It was Theodore Roosevelt and the First Volunteer Cavalry and the **Regular Army Ninth Cavalry** (an African-American regiment) that changed the tide of the day's events. At 12:30 that afternoon, Roosevelt led his men up the hill and pushed the Spaniards off it, despite suffering heavy casualties. By 1:30 p.m., the Americans had taken not only Kettle Hill but the entire San Juan ridge.

Four miles to the southeast, other American troops had a terrible time assaulting El Caney. The Spanish put up a heroic defense, and it was not until 4:00 p.m. that the Americans had captured the hill. Only 40 of the Spanish defenders managed to escape to Santiago, making the Spanish loss for the day 480 men, but the Americans had suffered 1,475 men killed, wounded or missing in the crowded labyrinth of terrain that lay in front of the San Juan ridge and El Caney ridges. The size of the American losses makes one ponder what might have happened if the Spanish had allocated even 1,000 men to the defense of the hills, instead of 521.

The day's fighting ensured the success of the American attack on Santiago, and the city surrendered on July 17. The United States had won a "splendid little war," and Lt. Colonel Theodore Roosevelt had won undying fame as the hero of the Battle of San Juan Hill.

Theodore Roosevelt

At the turn of the twentieth century, Japan was on its way to becoming a major power. Having been "opened" to trade with the West by the United States in 1854, Japan modernized its economy and military, and by 1904, the Japanese battle fleet was as equal to all others. In that year, Japan took the daring step of choosing to fight Czarist Russia for hegemony in **Korea** and **Manchuria**, areas that Russia had long desired because of its need for fresh water ports on the Pacific Ocean. The **Russo-Japanese War** (1904-1905) pitted the world's largest land power against a small island nation. Whether in population, industrial capacity, or size of armies, the Russians appeared to hold every advantage over the Japanese.

On February 8, 1904, Japanese **torpedo boats** entered the harbor of **Port Arthur** and shelled the Russian battleships there. It was a surprise attack, a prelude to **Pearl Harbor** 37 years later. The Russians lost two battleships and one cruiser in the night attack; a follow-up attack the next day claimed another Russian cruiser. The losses immediately put Russia on the defensive.

Japanese ground forces surrounded Port Arthur in the late summer of 1904 and began a series of courageous attacks on the city. The first ground assault took place from August 7 to 8; subsequent attacks were launched from August 19 to 25, September 15 to 30 and October 30 to November 1. All of these attacks were costly to the Japanese infantry, who attacked in suicidal waves, rushing Russian defenders manning machine guns. On December 5, the Japanese seized control of **203 Meter Hill**, overlooking the city and port.

From that position, they began to lob artillery shells into the city, and on January 2, 1905, Russian General **Anatoli M. Stesel** surrendered a force of 24,000 soldiers and 9,000 seamen. In the course of the siege, the Japanese lost 57,780 men killed, wounded or missing, while the Russians suffered 31,306 casualties. The siege anticipated the type of fighting that would prevail in **World War I**: stubborn defensive warfare, utilizing trenches and machine guns (the first machine gun, the Gatling gun, was patented in 1862; the Lewis gun, most used in World War I, was patented in 1911). The Japanese victory at Port Arthur also signaled a nearly fatal blow for Russian ambitions in the Pacific. From 1905 until 1945, it was Japanese ships, not Russian, that would dominate the waters between Japan and Asia.

Japanese machine gun position

By 1905, the Russians found that their massive resources could not be brought to bear against Japan; the Russian **Trans-Siberian railroad** was single-tracked and could not transport all the men and material necessary to fight the war. Czar **Nicholas II (1868-1918)** ordered the **Baltic Fleet**, the pride of the Russian navy, to sail from St. Petersburg, around Africa and Indonesia, to the Pacific to defeat the Japanese at sea.

The Russians departed from their home waters on October 15, 1904 with their decks filled with coal. The British, who controlled most of the refueling stations, were sympathetic to the Japanese. To make matters worse, the Russians ran into a fishing fleet off **Dover**, England and brought about an international controversy by firing at the boats.

When the Russians finally approached the **Sea of Japan**--the body of water separating Japan from Korea--they found the Japanese fleet waiting for them near **Tsushima Island.** Japanese Admiral **Heihachiro Togo (1847-1934)** completely outmaneuvered the Russians in the fighting. Twice the Japanese were able to "cross the T" of their enemy, meaning that the Japanese ships steamed across the top of the Russian line and fired broadsides into their foes. The Russians were unable to respond, as their artillery was not in position. Within a few hours the fighting was over. All but three of 37 Russian ships were captured by the Japanese, as was Russian Admiral **Zinovy P. Rozhdestvenski.** It was a complete disaster for the Russians who lost nearly all of their Baltic Fleet in one day. The battle greatly enhanced Japanese prestige around the world. For the first time, a non-Western power had defeated a Western one, using the equipment and tactics that had been developed in Europe by the British Navy over 100 years earlier. Togo truly became the "Japanese Nelson" and his victory brought Russia to the peace table. The negotiations were begun in Washington D.C., under the mediation of American President **Theodore Roosevelt**, and were moved to Portsmouth, New Hampshire, where the treaty was signed on September 5, 1905.

Czar Nicholas II

While Germany was seeking to crush France in the summer of 1914, Russia sent two large armies into East Prussia, hoping to defeat Germany. Czar **Nicholas II (1868-1918)** of Russia was a second cousin of Kaiser **Wilhelm II** of Germany, but their family ties did not prevent the **Romanov** and **Hohenzollern** dynasties from attempting a fight to the death.

The two Russian armies were commanded by Generals **Paveln Rennenkampf** and **Alexander Samsonov**, two men who had publicly feuded with each other during the **Russo-Japanese War** ten years earlier. Samsonov moved northward from Russian-held Poland while Rennenkampf moved westward from Lithuania. At first both armies met success; the German defenses were weak, since so many troops had been sent to participate in the **Battle for France** (see no. 84). Unnerved by the appearance of Russian troops in East Prussia, the German high command dispatched two infantry corps from the French front by railroad and sent Generals **Paul von Hindenberg (1847-1934)** and **Erich von Ludendorff (1865-1937)** to lead the defense in the east.

Von Hindenberg and Von Ludendorff

All factors favored the Russians, who had over a million men involved in the offensive, but Russia's lack of modernization proved costly. The two Russian commanders lacked an effective system of sending coded messages, so they resorted to sending clear messages across the wires. Thus the Germans learned everything they needed to know about the Russian troop composition and movements.

Knowing that Rennenkampf was moving slowly, the Germans struck swiftly to intercept and attack Samsonov's forces near the **Masurian Lakes**. A single German cavalry division was sent to further delay Rennenkampf's movements; the rest of the German army enveloped Samsonov's forces

by August 26, 1914.

The fighting that followed was fierce, but the Germans had the advantage of surprise. Using the mobility and communications that railroad and telegraph allowed, the Germans fought the Russians piecemeal, unit by unit. After four days of fighting, the Russians retreated, leaving 310,000 men dead or wounded and 90,000 prisoners. In the aftermath of the battle, Samsonov went into the woods and shot himself. Rennenkampf's army arrived too late to be of any use. Learning of the disaster, Rennenkampf retreated to the Lithuanian border, half-heartedly pursued by the Germans.

World War I began at **Sarajevo** in the Balkans, but it quickly spread to a full-scale war with Germany and Austria against France, England, Russia and the Low Countries (Holland and Belgium). Germany was determined to knock out the Low Countries and France during the summer of 1914. Two million German soldiers marched in five columns through the low countries and into France. As they headed toward Paris, the French became fearful, for they believed the loss of the capital city would end the bulk of resistance.

The Germans were weary from their long march (there were no jeeps or personnel carriers in World War I), and they slowed as they approached Paris. An Allied plane spotted a turn in the German

Coin commemorating the Battle of the Marne

line that afforded the possibility of a counterattack. On September 5, 1914, French and British soldiers launched their assault at the **Marne River**.

The fighting raged for five days. At first the Allies had the advantage, and they pushed the Germans back several miles. The Germans regrouped and resisted the Allied attacks. By the fourth day, the battle had disintegrated, and it was possible that either side might have collapsed under the strain. At a critical point, when the French lines were in danger of breaking, they were reinforced by several thousand men brought from Paris by taxicabs. The **Taxicab Army** provided the respite that enabled the French to hold their ground. By September 10, the Germans withdrew from the Marne sector, and gave up their goal of seizing Paris in that first campaign. The **Battle of the Marne** stopped the steady German advance.

A French soldier

After the battles of the **Marne** (see no. 78) and **Tannenburg**, (see no. 79), **World War I** slipped into a stalemate on both the eastern and western fronts. In early 1915, **Winston Churchill**, First Lord of the Admiralty **(1874-1965)** in Great Britain, devised a plan to break the deadlock. If the **Allied Powers** could use their strength at sea to capture **Constantinople**, the capital city of the Ottoman Empire, Allied fleets could then supply Russia with guns and ammunition by way of the Mediterranean and Black Sea shipping routes. If the Russians could be supplied with enough material, Churchill reasoned, the weight of the Russian numbers ought to be enough to defeat the Germans and end the war.

General **Sir Ian Hamilton (1853-1947)** commanded the 13 British and allied divisions, combined with a corps of French infantry, bringing the total to 490,000 men deployed during the campaign. The Allies made abortive attempts to force their ships through the passage of the **Dardanelles** in February and March. Following those early failures, in which the British lost a number of ships, Hamilton decided to capture the entire peninsula of **Gallipoli** before taking Constantinople. On April 25, 1915, Hamilton's troops went ashore at **Cape Helles** and **Anzac Cove**. The initial Allied landings were successful, but they found it nearly impossible to expand upon their beachheads. The Turks had been warned by the naval attempts to force the passage earlier, and had brought up large numbers of troops to hold the peninsula, perhaps 500,000 men in all.

British cannon and howitzers had little impact on the Turks, who were well-entrenched on high ground. As the British and their allies were unable to break out from their landing spots, the Turks rained

down a bombardment of their own upon the Allied positions. A stalemate soon developed, one that resembled the trench warfare that was going on in France and the Low Countries, the very situation that Churchill had hoped to avoid by fighting in the east.

It was clear by autumn that the entire operation was a failure. In December, the Allies began to withdraw their troops. By January 9, 1916, the last of the British, French and Australian troops had been removed, at a cost of 250,000 killed, wounded, or missing. The Turks had suffered a equal number of casualties. The operation became renowned in Australia as the first major demonstration of Australian troops in the field and **Anzac's Day** is still celebrated in Australia.

Sir Ian Hamilton

Just as the Allied Powers had tried to break the stalemate of **World War I** at **Gallipoli** (see no. 80) the Germans sought to make a breakthrough at **Verdun** in north-central France in 1916. The German leaders planned to make Verdun the point at which they would shatter the will of the French.

The Germans opened the campaign with heavy artillery bombardment. Bringing up troops rapidly by railroad, the Germans unleashed a ferocious assault on the forts surrounding the city of Verdun. **Fort Douaumont** fell to the attackers on February 24, and the French situation soon became critical.

Soldiers in Verdun

French Field Marshal **Joseph Joffre** sent General **Henri Petain (1856-1951)** to assume command of the defense. Petain encouraged his men with the famous phrase, "Ils ne passeront pas!" (They shall not pass!), and he widened the single road that was available to bring supplies and reinforcements into Verdun from the west. When the Germans resumed their attack, directing it against

Fort Vaux, they found the French ready for them. Although they were outnumbered, the French were masterful at rotating their divisions during the campaign, and many German assaults were made against fresh troops who had just been brought to the front. Still, the weight of the German fire and manpower began to be felt, and on June 6, Fort Vaux fell to the Germans.

So many troops had been lost in the effort to take Fort Vaux, that the Germans relied heavily upon artillery bombardment rather than frontal attacks. The summer of 1916 found the ground in and around the city scarred from thousands of shells fired by both sides. The German attacks began to lessen as autumn approached, and on October 24, French General **Robert Neveille** (who had succeeded Petain) launched a series of counterattacks that drove the Germans back. The French recaptured Fort Douaumont on October 24 and Fort Vaux on November 2. The battlefield quieted 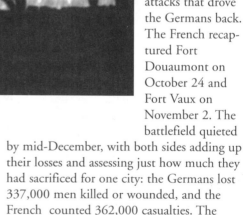 by mid-December, with both sides adding up their losses and assessing just how much they had sacrificed for one city: the Germans lost 337,000 men killed or wounded, and the French counted 362,000 casualties. The enormous battle had gained nothing for either side, and the deadly stalemate of World War I continued.

As **World War I** continued, no one seemed to have found the answer to the deadlock imposed by trench warfare. British General **Sir Douglas Haig (1861-1928)** believed, as did many of his colleagues, that it would take a concentration of superior firepower and British troops to break through the German lines.

On July 1, 1916, the cream of the British army advanced against German positions that had just endured five days of continuous bombardment; over 1,700,000 shells had been fired against the German lines. The British troops who moved forward that day were men who had been raised with the conviction that Britain was invincible; after all, during the nineteenth century, **Queen Victoria's** army had controlled over one-fifth of the world's surface with only 200,000 men in uniform. As the British advanced, they ran into devastating small arms fire from the Germans, who had protected themselves effectively during the five-day bombardment.

Fighting from their entrenched positions, the Germans took a tremendous toll on the oncoming British troops that first day of fighting: 57,474 British soldiers were killed, wounded, missing or captured by the day's end. That battle toll was

Field Marshal Sir Douglas Haig

greater than the total casualties the Victorian army had suffered in its battles in Africa, India and Southeast Asia during the previous century.

Although the **Somme** campaign lasted months longer, the British and their French allies never attacked with such confidence again. Indeed, their timidity at times inspired the Germans to come forth in ill-considered counterattacks that cost them a great number of casualties. By the time the fighting came to an end in November, the British had lost 418,000 men, the French 194,000, and the Germans 650,000. It was a staggering total for three armies, especially on such a narrow front, where the deepest penetration made by either side over months of fighting came to only three miles.

German trench and wire at the Somme

American and French soldiers in the Meuse-Argonne

As late as September 1918, it was not certain that Imperial Germany would surrender to the Allied Powers. It was also not clear whether the American troops brought to fight in France would remain under U.S. control or be parceled out among French and British regiments. Both questions were answered by the Allied performance during the battle of the **Meuse River** and **Argonne forest**.

Then, American Colonel **George C. Marshall (1880-1959)**, directed the tremendous effort that brought 600,000 American troops, 3,980 heavy guns, and 90,000 horses into position, while 220,000 French and Italian troops were removed from the area. On September 26, General **John Pershing's (1860-1948) American First Army** and the **French Fourth Army** of General **Henri Gouraud (1867-1946)**, began a series of attacks on the German positions over a 35-mile stretch of front west of Verdun, extending north from the Argonne forest to the city of **Sedan**. The Americans attacked with troops and 189 light tanks; the French had 300 tanks.

The advance on the first day of fighting was only two to three miles, and the Germans quickly brought up fresh divisions of troops to defend the area. By September 30, the Franco-American attacks had gained an average of only eight miles, but they had taken 18,000 prisoners and 200 heavy guns from the enemy. The Allied powers then paused, while the Germans continued to transfer troops, both to meet the Argonne offensive and to counter British attacks in the north.

The Franco-American attacks resumed on October 4. German High Commander **Eric von Ludendorff (1865-1937)** motivated the Germans to fight with spirit, although they were outnumbered by as many as six to one on some parts of the front. The Americans advanced only one mile in three days on their right flank, and three miles in two days on their left. The second phase of the battle ground to a halt around October 14, with many of the Allied objectives as yet unfulfilled.

The third and final phase of the offensive began on November 1, when the American First and French Fourth armies resumed their attacks. By November 4, the Germans were in full retreat from the area. The French Fourth Army closed in on the town of **Mezieres**, a junction on a vital east-west railway. The American Army reached Sedan by November 11, the day the Armistice was signed. The Americans had committed a total of 1,200,000 men to the battle, losing 117,000 killed or wounded; the Germans lost 126,000 men killed or wounded.

The American performance in the battle showed that the **doughboys** were as good as the British Tommies, French poilus, Australian Anzacs, and Germans.

BATTLE FOR FRANCE
May 10 - June 25, 1940

The German people never forgot the humiliating losses they suffered during **World War I** and the terms they conceded to in the **Treaty of Versailles** in 1919. When **Adolf Hitler (1889-1945)** promised to lead Germany into a new glorious age, a **Third Reich** in the tradition of the Holy Roman Empire, many Germans were ready to follow him.

After conquering **Poland** in the fall of 1939, Hitler paused for several months, and newspapers that winter referred to his campaign as the **Phony War**. All was quiet until Hitler struck again in the spring of 1940.

On April 25, 1940, German soldiers, tanks, personnel carriers, jeeps, and Volkswagens moved into the dense **Ardennes** forest in northeast France, avoiding the formidable defenses of the **Maginot Line**. Thinking that the forest was impassable to motorized forces, the French had only a light screen of infantry troops guarding the area. To their astonishment, they were pushed back by the combination of German forces. The speed and force of the attack characterized what would soon become known as a **Blitzkrieg,** meaning lightning warfare, where one side struck so hard and fast that the opponent had no time to regroup or fall back.

The German Blitzkrieg pushed through

Hitler in Paris

the forest in a matter of days and emerged on the other side, poised to conquer the Low Countries of Holland and Belgium. The **British Expeditionary Force** (B.E.F.), supporting the French, retreated to the French and Belgian coast, trying to reach England. Some 338,000 British and French troops were evacuated from **Dunkirk** by British fishing vessels, transport carriers, and even private yachts and sailboats. The British answer to the Blitzkreig was a brilliant evacuation that saved a large number of troops.

As for France, the worst was still to come. German forces entered Paris on June 12, and the French were pushed further south. Field Marshall **Henri Petain (1856-1951)** (see no. 81) was called out of retirement to negotiate an armistice with the Germans. Petain arranged for France to retain control of the lower third of the country, with a new government centered at the city of **Vichy**, instead of Paris. To the French, the battle had been a terrific disaster and the sight of Paris in the hands of the Germans was an unbearable humiliation. Two hundred thousand Frenchmen had been killed or wounded in the fighting. Hitler celebrated by having the armistice signed in the same railway car that the Allies had forced peace upon the Germans in 1918.

Adolf Hitler (1889-1945) was willing, indeed eager, to come to terms with Great Britain. But **Winston Churchill (1874-1965)**, who had become **Prime Minister** on May 10, 1940, was indomitable in his resistance. He would never surrender and never negotiate with the Nazi power, thus, Hitler decided to conquer Britain.

The Germans were well aware that no foreign power had taken England since the year 1066, and that **Louis XIV** and **Napoleon Bonaparte** had each failed because of Britain's command of the sea. Now, German power in the air, represented by the **Luftwaffe** (the German air force) was thought to be sufficient to bomb the British people into surrender. Hitler ordered the Luftwaffe to conduct bombing campaigns over Britain to warm up for **Operation Sea Lion,** a full-scale invasion

London under attack

of Britain if that should prove necessary. The battle began on August 13, known as the **Day of the Eagle**, with the attack of 1,485 German aircraft.

What Hitler had failed to acknowledge was the British development of a new weapon: **radar**. The British would learn in advance where the German bombing attacks were headed, and they would send fighter planes from the **Royal Air Force** (R.A.F.) into the air to combat the oncoming German fighters and bombers. Even so, the weight of the German offensives was enough to allow the Germans considerable success. They bombed a number of British airfields and were on their way toward subduing the R.A.F. when Hitler ordered a change in strategy. Rather than demolish the airfields, he ordered the Luftwaffe to concentrate on reducing the major British cities to rubble. German planes soon converged on **London** and **Coventry** and wreaked havoc on the urban population of Great Britain.

The steadfastness of the British people during the **Blitz** was remarkable. Inspired by Winston Churchill's radio broadcasts, heartened by the knowledge that the R.A.F. was striking back against the Germans, and filled with a determination to overcome, the British waited it out. Many people spent their nights in subway tunnels in London and bomb shelters. Meanwhile, the strength of the R.A.F. continued to grow as did the accuracy of its radar detection. By September 17, 1940, the Germans were suffering more losses in the air than they could afford, and Hitler pulled back from the battle. It was his first serious defeat, and its implications would become larger as the war went on. Churchill exulted over the victory, praising the pilots of the R.A.F. with his famous words, "Never in the field of human conflict was so much owed by so many to so few."

While Germany and Italy were fighting against Russia and Great Britain, the United States was still on the sidelines. A strong isolationist movement remained from the losses suffered in **World War I**, and many Americans hoped they could remain out of another European war. That attitude changed when the American naval base at **Pearl Harbor**, Hawaii was atacked.

Imperial Japan had joined in a defensive treaty with Germany and Italy. Having succeeded in over running much of China in the 1930s, the Japanese were looking for new fields to conquer. President **Franklin Roosevelt (1882-1945)** of the United States declared an embargo on the sale of oil supplies to Japan in 1941, as a way to register American displeasure with Japanese conquests in East Asia. Soon after that embargo was declared, the Japanese military government began to plan a deadly surprise attack against the United States.

Although American intelligence personnel warned that the Japanese posed a threat, most policy makers discounted danger from the east. It was believed the Japanese were not skillful or reckless enough to engage the United States. Americans were stunned when the Japanese carried out a sneak attack early Sunday morning, December 7, 1941.

A Japanese fleet commanded by Admiral **Chuichi Nagumo** had left Japan and steamed on a course that brought it to the northeast of the **Hawaiian Islands**. Holding the advantage of surprise, the Japanese airplanes took off from their carriers and struck the U.S. base at 7:55 a.m. The results were devastating for the Americans: 188 planes were destroyed in the attack and 2,581 Americans were killed. Five of the eight battleships in the harbor were sunk, but none of the **Pacific Fleet** carriers were hit; they were at sea when the attack came. The attack was over in an hour. The Japanese had struck a powerful and effective blow against the Americans, but their failure to destroy the carriers proved costly. As Japanese High Admiral **Isoruku Yamamoto (1884-1943)** had predicted, Japan could fight the U.S. on equal terms for a time before American industrial might outproduced and overwhelmed the island nation. Pearl Harbor became a rallying cry for Americans, and millions rushed to enlist in the armed forces. The days of isolationism were over, and the United States entered the war against Japan. Then, Germany declared war on the United States on December 11, 1941.

USS Shaw explodes in Pearl Harbor

Japanese High Admiral **Isoruku Yamamoto (1884-1943)** informed his superiors that he needed to win another important victory in the Pacific to ensure that the Americans would not bomb the home islands of Japan. In May 1942, Yamamoto steamed forth from Japan with four carriers, several battleships and a host of supporting ships that totaled 162 vessels; the largest and strongest

Navy fighters attack at Midway

fleet Japan would place in action during the war. Yamamoto steamed toward **Midway Island**, hoping to catch the Americans by surprise once again.

In the six months since **Pearl Harbor** (see no. 86), a small team of American radio experts had succeeded in breaking the Japanese code. Working day and night from basement quarters in Hawaii, the team relayed critical information about Yamamoto's movements to admirals **Raymond Spruance**

and **Frank Jack Fletcher**. As the Japanese approached Midway Island, two American fleets were ready to meet them.

The battle raged from June 4 through June 6, 1942, with the critical fighting on the morning of June 4. The Japanese launched 108 planes at 6:30 a.m.; the planes hit Midway Island with some success. A large number of American bomber planes struck back against the Japanese fleet; 33 torpedo planes were lost, and no impact was made upon the Japanese. The turning point came when 54 **Dauntless**, United States dive bombers, were launched at 10:26 a.m. Finding the Japanese fleet, the Americans descended just as hundreds of Japanese planes were refueling on the decks of three carriers. For five crucial minutes, the American planes bombed the Japanese ships, and in those five minutes, the naval war for supremacy in the Pacific was lost for Japan. Numerous planes and experienced pilots were wiped out, three carriers were sunk and the fourth was badly damaged. As the Japanese limped away from the air battles at Midway, Admiral Yamamoto knew, though many of the Japanese high command would deny, that Japan had made her bid to win the war and failed.

Field Marshall **Erwin Rommel (1891-1944)** was one of the most dynamic of the German military leaders in **World War II**. Often seen in a Volkswagen, scouting terrain in advance of his tank columns, Rommel became a symbol of German daring and was respected even by Allied soldiers.

By June 1942 Rommel had succeeded in capturing the fortified city of **Tobruk**, Libya, and his tanks were pointed directly toward the British-held city of **Alexandria**, Egypt. If Rommel took Alexandria and came to control Egypt, then Hitler would be able to shut off the **Suez Canal**, threatening Great Britain's oil supply. Rommel pushed ahead toward Egypt.

He was met at **El Alamein** by British General **Claude Auchinleck**, in command of 20,000 men and 252 tanks. Rommel had fewer tanks than the British and his supplies were scarce, but his famed **Afrika Korps** was confident of victory. Rommel battled with the British forces for several days but was unable to penetrate their lines. Auchinleck had chosen a favorable site for the battle: 60 miles to the west of Alexandria, El Alemain lay between the Mediterranean to the north and the **Qatarra Depression** to the south, leaving Rommel little room to maneuver. By July 27, the battle had disintegrated into a stalemate, leaving the British with the advantage of being closer to their supply base in Alexandria.

Auchinleck was replaced by General **Bernard Montgomery (1887-1976)**, a care-

General Bernard Montgomery

ful planner, who slowly built up his forces during the summer and early fall. In October, Montgomery launched a series of attacks on the German positions. Knowing that Rommel was short on fuel, Montgomery carried out a series of "staggered" attacks that changed location as soon as the German reserves came into action. The German armored reserves began to run out of fuel in rushing from battle to battle, and the Italian infantry units began to break under the strain. Following a major but inconclusive tank battle on November 2, Rommel began to withdraw. He was hampered by the desire of Hitler to hold the position, but Rommel managed to extricate many of his men without further losses. The British were slow to exploit their success, but when they did advance into Libya, they found the German resistance greatly weakened. Rommel's daring had not enabled the Germans to win strategic control in North Africa.

German troops in Russia

Taking on the bear of Mother Russia was a formidable task and only leaders as megalomaniac as **Napoleon Bonaparte (1769-1821)** and **Adolf Hitler (1889-1945)** were likely to do so. **Operation Barbarossa,** launched on June 22, 1941, initiated the greatest spree of killing ever known in a single front. German troops streamed into Russia, and using their famed tactics of **Blitzkrieg** (see no. 84) managed to come close to **Moscow** in December, before they were halted by a series of Russian counterattacks.

In the spring of 1942, Hitler launched a new offensive. Wanting to take and hold the oil-rich areas in the Caucasus Mountains, he sent large sections of the German forces in Russia toward the **Crimean Peninsula** and the city of **Stalingrad**, named for the leader of Soviet Russia, **Joseph Stalin (1879-1953)**. The Germans headed straight for the oil fields, but Hitler-- who was increasingly taking over control from his generals--insisted the armies first take and hold Stalingrad.

The Germans entered the suburbs of the city in August, and began a fierce series of battles to take possession. The main Russian army remained on the east bank of the **Volga River**, not entering the defense, which was conducted by the people of the city and a garrison of soldiers. In the hand-to-hand street fighting that ensued, the German principles of speed and maneuver were far less effective than they had been on the open ground of the Russian steppes. Three months of bloody fighting gave the Germans control of ninety percent of the city, but at the cost of a great number of men.

The Russians struck back on November 19, 1942, in a broad circular series of attacks across the Don and Volga rivers. The Russians brushed aside the Hungarian and Rumanian units guarding the German flanks, and in two weeks they had completely encircled the German **Sixth Army** within the ruined city. General **Friedrich von Paulus** asked for permission to break out of the trap he was in, but Hitler assured him the German air force would resupply him by plane. With no option but to continue to fight, von Paulus and his men stayed, even when a relief unit from the Crimean Peninsula came within 30 miles of the city. The German air force was unable to live up to its promise of delivering supplies, and by late January the Germans inside the city were starving. Von Paulus sent word to Hitler, asking for permission to surrender; the response he received was the baton of a Prussian field marshal. Hitler's message was to fight to the death. Instead, von Paulus chose to surrender, and by February 2, 1943, the remaining 70,000 German soldiers gave themselves up to the Russian forces.

German Tiger tank

The greatest tank battle ever fought took place on rolling terrain near **Prokorovka**, Russia. The battle itself was inconclusive, but the campaign that it was part of, **Kursk**, was one of the most decisive actions of **World War II**.

In the spring of 1943 **Adolf Hitler (1889-1945)** contemplated one more offensive on the Russian front, hoping to counter the disaster at **Stalingrad** (see no. 89) and the loss of the **Sixth Army**. Russian advances during the winter and spring had created a bulge 70 miles long and 100 miles wide in the middle of the front, into the German defensive lines. Hitler reasoned that hammer-like blows on both edges of the salient, or bulge, might produce the resounding victory he needed to regain the morale of his men and country. The Germans commenced their attacks on the bulge near the city of Kursk on July 5, 1943.

Russian intelligence had been well ahead of the Germans. Knowing that severe attacks would take place in that area, the Russians had created three belts of defenses on both the northern and southern ends of the bulge. The German attack coming from the north was stopped dead in its tracks. The attack

from the south almost succeeded in breaking through the Russian defenses, but there were plenty of Russian reserves to throw into the gaps. Not only did the Russians have more men available, but their factories (which Stalin had moved hundreds of miles to beyond the **Ural Mountains**) were producing far more planes and tanks than the Germans. The Russians had air superiority throughout the battle, and their **T-34** tank was a much superior model to its predecessors; only the German **Tiger** tank was better, and the Germans had relatively few of these available at Kursk.

The enormous tank battle was fought on July 12, between 700 German tanks of the **Fourth Panzer Army** and 850 tanks of the Russian **Fifth Guards Tank Army**. Men and machines rolled through the terrain for hours, causing death and destruction on both sides, but neither side emerged as the clear winner.

The battle might well have been ruled a draw except for the fact that Hitler needed to pull armored units out of Russia to protect the Italian coast from Allied landings. Hitler's decision weakened the German lines to the extent that Germany never held the initiative again on the Russian front.

From 1941 through 1944, **Joseph Stalin (1879-1953)** continually insisted that the British and Americans open a "second front" in Europe to take pressure off his beleaguered Soviet forces. Due to a need to build up troop strength in England and coordinate efforts, the British and Americans were not ready to invade the continent until early 1944, and even then many of their leaders entertained serious apprehensions. German leader **Adolf Hitler (1889-1945)** had taken the continent so decisively during 1940 and 1941 that many of the British generals were terrified of a rematch.

The go-ahead came from American General **Dwight D. Eisenhower (1890-1969)**, Supreme Commander of the Allied Forces. When he was informed by weathermen that the Channel crossing would be unpredictable in early June, he thought for several moments and then uttered his famous line, "Okay, let's go." The time for waiting had passed; it was time to strike a blow

General Dwight D. Eisenhower

against the Germans on the Continent. During the night of June 5, 1,213 warships, 4,126 landing ships, 763 ancillary vessels and 864 merchant ships were deployed between Plymouth, England, and the **Normandy** coast of France. Airborne troops landed in the German rear and cut bridges and communications. A ferocious bombing was used to soften German positions. In spite of all this preparation, there was still a great deal of uncertainty when 175,000 American, British, Canadian and Australian troops headed toward their landing points that morning of June 6.

The Allied troops hit the beaches at 6:30 a.m. and were met by a surprising level of fire from the German defenders. The Germans had expected the main attack to take place in the **Pas de Calais** region, yet the defenders on the beaches fought with ferocity. The Americans landed on two beaches they named **Utah** and **Omaha**; they penetrated to a depth of nine miles on the former, but were held to an enclave of only 1.5 miles on Omaha at a cost of 3,000 casualties. The British landed at **Gold** and **Sword** beaches and pulled to within sight of the towns of **Bayeux** and **Caen** on the first day. Canadian soldiers landed at **Juno** and penetrated inland to a depth of seven miles.

The Germans were handicapped in their defensive fighting, since Hitler had ordered the armored units not to move without his orders; by the time the Fuhrer was roused in his bunker at 4:00 p.m., it was too late for the German counterattack to have any significant effect. By nightfall on June 6, the Allies had put ashore 87,000 men and 7,000 vehicles. Given the Allied superiority in the air, there was no chance the Germans could dislodge those men from their hard-won beachheads on the Normandy coast. Hitler's **Fortress Europe** had been delivered a great blow.

Few world leaders have been as audacious as **Adolf Hitler (1889-1945)**. Even as Russian, American and British armies were converging on the soil of Germany itself, he planned a last, desperate attack that had a chance of splitting the Allies in the west and buying some time to confront the Russians in the east. The result of Hitler's gamble was the **Battle of the Bulge**, fought at the end of the year 1944, in the same **Ardennes** forest that the Germans had pushed through in the spring of 1940 when they won the **Battle of France** (see no. 84).

On December 16, under cover of darkness, German units attacked the thin American line defending the Ardennes forest. At first the Americans fell back in confusion, some units even fighting with each other in the darkness. By morning the Germans had opened the start of a bulge or salient, pointed toward the city of **Bastogne**, the **Meuse River**, and ultimately **Antwerp**, the major center of supplies for the Allied armies.

The dreaded SS storm troopers of the Nazi army moved in the lead, scoring important gains early on in the battle. The Germans were helped in the first week of the battle by the fact that overcast weather prevented effective Allied air coverage. The Germans pushed on toward their goal to cross the Meuse River.

Although there was some panic at Allied

Heavily armed German soldier

headquarters, General **Dwight D. Eisenhower (1890-1969)** was confident the Allies could stop the German attack. Overall battlefield command in the Ardennes area was given to British General **Bernard Montgomery (1887-1976)**, while command of the American forces in the south and west were under the command of American General **George Patton (1885-1945)**. The key point to be held was the city of Bastogne, through which strategic railroad lines and roads crisscrossed. The Germans surrounded the city and demanded its surrender. The American commander, General **Anthony McAuliffe**, replied with one word--"Nuts!" His determination to hold the city was rewarded on December 26, when General Patton's **Third Army** arrived to relieve the defenders. The skies also cleared, allowing Allied planes to commence the bombardment of advancing German tanks. Hitler's gamble had come close--German tanks got within ten miles of the Meuse River. While it is unlikely that Germany's defeat could have been staved off for long, the offensive had the potential to discourage the Allies and prolong the war. Instead, the German losses suffered during the month of fighting in the Ardennes forest (100,000 men and 800 tanks) ensured the war would end sooner rather than later.

As American ships and planes came closer to the soil of **Imperial Japan**, the Japanese resistance became more fierce. The Americans wanted to take the island of **Iwo Jima** to use as a base for sending planes directly against the mainland of Japan. Knowing the Japanese were planning an extensive defense of the island, the Americans tried to soften up the defenders with aerial and ship bombardments. The total weight of the artillery that hammered the island was so great that American invaders on February 19, 1945 expected little resistance.

Led by General **Todomichi Kuribyashi**, the 22,000 Japanese defenders had secured themselves within tunnels and fortifications, and they were ready to fight when the Americans came ashore. The Japanese showed their hand at the last possible moment, opening up their fire just as the American boats were unloading their troops. Had the Japanese fired earlier, they would have inflicted even greater losses upon the invaders. As it was, the Americans fought their way ashore despite heavy casualties that first day. There followed a series of ambushes, raids, and counterattacks, with the Americans steadily rooting out the Japanese, but suffering considerable losses in the process. On February 23, the American flag was mounted on **Mount Surubachi**, an event that has since been commemorated in film and literature.

The actual fighting raged on until March 16. The Japanese fought like tigers in a cage and when the battle was truly over, only 212 Japanese had chosen to surrender. The rest of the garrison had died, as did 6,891 Americans, along with 18,700 wounded.

U.S. flag waves over Iwo Jima

Russian flag raised on the Reichstag

In his time of conquest, Geman leader **Adolf Hitler (1889-1945)** and his armies had taken the capital cities of many peoples: Rotterdam, Paris, Belgrade, Athens and others. The loss of **Berlin** to the oncoming Russian soldiers was a justified blow to the leaders of the **Third Reich**, and it signaled the end of Hitler's dream of world conquest.

The Russians deployed two and a half million men in two armies that encircled Berlin. Commanded by Field Marshals **Georgi Zhukov** and **Ivan Konev**, the Russians smashed through the German **Central Army Group** and advanced on the city itself. The city was defended by as many as 700,000 men under arms, but the majority of these were militia forces, many comprised of boys ten to sixteen years of age. These were the forces with which Hitler would defend the last remnants of the Third Reich!

Hitler issued commands from his underground bunker in the center of Berlin. There was fierce German resistance: it took four days of bloody street fighting for the two different Russian armies to break through the defenders to link up in the center of the city. By that time, Hitler had committed suicide in his bunker. The German parliamentary building, the **Reichstag**, symbol of German greatness, fell on May 1, and on the following day German General **Helmuth Weidling**, commander of the Berlin garrison, surrendered his remaining 135,000 troops to the Russians. The Soviet flag flew over the Reichstag and the **Brandenburg Gate**, at a cost of 700,000 Russian casualties. Those German troops who were not included in the surrender made their way west as fast as possible, hoping to surrender to the Americans and British rather than to the Russians.

MacArthur observes shelling at Inchon

Tenth Corps of American Marines went ashore at the beaches of **Inchon**, 150 miles north of the front. In overall command of the operation, MacArthur watched while the Marines and other U.N. troops carried out one of the most daring amphibious movements in the history of warfare. United Nations ships landed 25,040 men that day, who took over the area with almost no opposition. There were no forces to oppose them, since North Korea had committed all its strength to the southern battlefields around the Pusan perimeter.

The start of the **Korean War** took both Americans and Europeans by surprise. It was a great disappointment to the Allies that the alliance forged in **World War II** with Soviet Russia could not be maintained. Only five years after the war, with the attack of Communist North Korea on South Korea, it seemed likely that American and British troops might fight against their former allies.

By late summer, American, British and other troops were fighting in South Korea, under the auspices of the **United Nations** (U.N.). The U.N.-South Korean cause was desperate, since the North Koreans had penetrated far into the peninsula. They had overrun and captured the capital city of **Seoul** early on in the campaign, and now they threatened to take all of South Korea.

General **Douglas MacArthur (1880-1964)** of the United States section of the United Nations forces proposed a radical solution: go on the offensive by landing behind and to the north of the invading North Korean forces. On September 15, 1950, the

The U.N. troops to the south made a breakout from the Pusan area the same day that MacArthur's men landed at Inchon. Learning of the American landing in the north and seeing the breakout, the North Korean forces began to disintegrate. Thousands of North Koreans deserted or were routed from their positions as the U.N. troops began a drive north. Seoul was liberated on September 27, and the U.N. forces reached the **38th parallel** of latitude by the end of the month. South Korea had been saved from a Communist takeover at a cost of 3,500 U.N. casualties; the North Koreans suffered 13,666 deaths and 4,692 captured.

MacArthur's action at Inchon allowed for a remarkable comeback by the United Nations forces. By preventing Communist domination of South Korea, MacArthur's men had made a strong statement about U.N. resolve to contain Communism in the post-World War II world.

Vietnam became a quagmire for two Western powers: France and the United States. When **World War II** ended, France attempted to hold onto the colonial empire it had built up in Southeast Asia. French imperialism ran into determined resistance by the people of North Vietnam, who followed **Ho Chi Minh(1890-1969)** in their struggle to push the French out and liberate their country.

France had many advantages when the war began, but the brilliant strategy of Vietnamese leaders such as General **Vo Nguyen Giap (b. 1912)** neutralized those advantages. By 1953, the French had concentrated their best fighting troops in the city of **Dien Bien Phu**, inland to the west of Hanoi. The French had 18,000 men there, the cream of the strategic reserve.

Some 37,000 North Vietnamese troops surrounded the French at Dien Bien Phu. The French were confident their air force could supply the fortress with food and ammunition. French planes flew 10,400 missions in support of the stronghold. But the Vietnamese brought up heavy artillery and antiaircraft weapons, and the French soon began to lose more planes than they could afford. The Vietnamese softened up the defenses with intense artillery bombardments through the winter of 1953 to 1954 and then on March 14, 1954, they began a series of deadly attacks, meant to capture the outlying positions and destroy the French morale. Although the Vietnamese sustained numerous casualties in their attacks, they seized one stronghold after another, and by April 24, the French had only 5,300 men still able to fight. The Vietnamese made one last major attack on May 7; the French surrendered the next day. The French had hoped that the United States might assist them, and it appears that President **Dwight D. Eisenhower (1890-1969)** considered, but rejected, using nuclear weapons to deter the Vietnamese. Over 12,000 French soldiers had died, while the Vietnamese suffered 22,900 men killed or wounded, but the morale boost for the Vietnamese was significant. The French agreed to a cease-fire on July 21, 1954.

The Vietnamese victory stood as a symbol of the determination of the Vietnamese Communists, and the approaching end of the long era of European domination of native peoples.

Communist suspect is questioned by French Foreign Legion

The terrain of the **Golan Heights**, lodged between **Syria** and **Israel**, seemed to prohibit Israeli takeover. The high ground on its northern border had been a hotspot for rocket attacks and guerrilla warfare by Syrian attackers. On June 6, 1967, the **Six Day War** broke out between Israel and its Arab neighbors. Swiftly winning command of the skies, the Israelis were able to deliver their attacks against the Egyptians, Jordanians and Syrians while being protected by their own air force. This was especially important on the northern front, where the Syrians controlling the Golan Heights appeared to have a substantial advantage over the Israelis who had to attack upward from the **Plain of Galilee**.

What no foreign observer-American, Russian or European-had guessed at was the quality and drive of the **Israeli Defense Forces**. Having grown up for an entire generation with the threat of war--and the reality of war in 1948 and 1956--the Israelis were ready for attack at any time.

The going was toughest on the Golan Heights. The Israelis used helicopter raids to seize key checkpoints and then advanced with tanks and bulldozers against the Syrians. After the bulldozers cleared away obstacles erected by the Syrians, the tanks moved forth into the heights and confronted the Syrians in a series of tank battles. Whether the fighting was tank to tank, or infantryman to soldier, the Israelis consistently did better. After two days of fierce conflict, the Syrians withdrew from the heights, having suffered 2,500 men killed and another 5,000 wounded. They also left behind over 100 tanks and 200 artillery pieces. The Israelis lost 115 men and women killed and 306 wounded, a significant number to the small Jewish state, but a low price to pay for having gained the strategic high ground between the two countries.

Israeli soldiers in a Merkava tank

The United States was the second Western capitalist power that sought to prevent Communist **North Vietnam** from overrunning **South Vietnam**. France had tried to hold on to its imperial stronghold in Vietnam and failed. The United States stepped into Southeast Asia in the early 1960's and slowly but surely committed itself to a war of attrition against the Communist and nationalist guerrilla fighters of the north.

In early 1968, the North Vietnamese leaders executed a huge offensive against the major towns and cities of South Vietnam, intended to persuade the population into joining the cause of the North. On January 29, 1968, the start of the New Year in Indochina, some 67,000 **North Vietnamese Army** (NVA) regulars attacked 36 of the 44 provincial capitals of South Vietnam. Using their best guerrilla tactics, the North Vietnamese fighters made some inroads, but were consistently thrown back by a combination of United States and South Vietnamese fighters. The offensive trailed off by mid-February and then renewed itself on February 18, when the **Viet Cong** launched mortar and rocket fire against 37 towns and cities. Within a few days, the North Vietnamese offensive had spent itself completely. The people of South Vietnam had not joined in a revolution against their leaders. The North Vietnamese had suffered tremendous casualties: 45,000 men are estimated to have been killed or wounded in the offensive, which cost the United States 1,829 men killed and 7,746 wounded; the South Vietnamese suffered 2,788 men killed and 8,299 wounded. On paper, there was no question that North Vietnam had suffered a

Viet Cong attack during Tet holiday

costly defeat.

The affair was perceived differently by American camera crews and American households who watched the nightly television broadcasts. Prior to the offensive, a slim majority of Americans had favored continued prosecution of the war; after the offensive, the tables turned, and a majority of Americans began to agree that it was time to reduce the American commitment to the Vietnamese struggle. American President **Lyndon B. Johnson (1908-1972)** may also have been a distant casualty of the offensive; rejected by his own party in the New Hampshire primary, he bowed out of any bid for reelection in 1968.

The Arab countries ached for revenge against **Israel** after the humiliations they suffered in the **Six Day War** in 1967. During 1973, Egypt and Syria agreed on coordinating an attack against Israel. The Egyptians and Syrians employed sophisticated camouflage of their men and equipment, and the Israeli high command did not respond to the last-minute warning signals it received. The Arab attacks on October 6 came as a surprise to the Israeli soldier on the ground.

The Egyptians mounted a crossing of the **Suez Canal** from **Port Said** in the north to **Suez City** in the south, with 285,000 Egyptian soldiers, who used pontoon bridges to bring across some 2,000 tanks. The Israelis were still confident of victory because of the longtime superiority of their air force, but when the first Israeli planes attacked the Arab lines, they lost large numbers of aircraft to the fire from handheld **Sam-6** missiles that many

Egyptian soldiers carried. By October 8, the Egyptians had crossed the canal and held their new positions against counterattacks by both land and air.

Unfamiliar to this type of success, the Egyptian commanders became cautious, delaying crucial hours before moving against the mountain passes to the east. Once they did seek to take the **Malta** and **Giddi** passes, their armor was turned back by a strong Israeli defense. The Egyptians paused on October 10 to wait for the cease-fire they expected.

Instead, they were counterattacked by the Israelis who on October 16 managed to slip through a weak link in the Egyptian lines. The Israelis crossed the canal to the west bank and knocked out Egyptian antiaircraft weapons, allowing the Israeli air force to dominate the front. When a cease-fire was called on October 24, it could be argued that the Egyptians were in a worse position than they had been back in 1967, at the end of the Six Day War, but their early success in crossing the canal had its effect. From that time forward, the Israelis never took their Arab foes lightly again, and a peace initiative began to develop, pressured by both the United States and the Soviet Union.

Egyptian troops

In August 1990, **Saddham Hussein (b. 1937)**, the dictator of **Iraq**, sent his army south to invade and occupy oil-rich **Kuwait**. Hussein's million-man army was successful in its campaign, but Iraq's aggression drew the wrath of President **George Bush (b.1924)** of the United States. Proceeding under a **United Nations** mandate to free Kuwait, Bush organized an enormous coalition of allies and dispatched hundreds of thousands of American troops to **Saudi Arabia**, where they took up positions opposite the Iraqi troops inside Kuwait. Following a series of dead-end attempts at negotiation, Bush authorized American General **H. Norman Schwartzkopf (b. 1934)** to attack and destroy the Iraqi army inside Kuwait.

Patriot missile launched to intercept Iraqi scud

A month-long aerial bombardment of both **Baghdad**, the capital of Iraq, and Kuwait, proceeded the Allied attack. Thousands of allied planes bombed and strafed the Iraqi positions; there was no answer from the Iraqi air force which was effectively grounded from the start of the air war. American-made **smart bombs** were reputed to be able to bomb military installations while leaving nearby civilian areas unharmed. Even given the overwhelming American strength in the air, Hussein refused to negotiate and held his army in its positions in Kuwait.

The allied attack on the ground began on February 24, 1991. Developed by General Schwartzkopf, the allied attack swept around the right wing of the Iraqis into the desert and then came back to fall upon their right rear. Fast-moving tank columns of the allies wreaked damage on their Iraqi opponents while American planes bombed convoys of retreating Iraqi troops. The Iraqi retreat soon turned into a rout, with hundreds of thousand of soldiers trying to escape from the bombs and tanks of the allied forces. Hussein's vaunted **Republican Guard** troops were among the first to flee; they were pursued to the Iraqi border by American tank columns. By February 28, the allied forces had won one of the most one-sided battles of modern times; 60,000 Iraqis had been killed and 175,000 taken prisoner in actions that cost the allied troops no more than 500 casualties.

Kuwait was liberated and the allies had shown what a combination of air power, strategic planning, and superior technology could accomplish. However, Saddam Hussein still remained in power in Iraq.

TRIVIA QUIZ & GAMES

Test your knowledge and challenge your friends with the following questions. The answers are on the pages noted.

1. In 52 BC this military leader pursued Vercingetorix and his army of 70,000 Gaul warriors to the fortress of Alesia, where he ordered his army to build two walls around the fortress - the inner wall was 11 miles around and the outer wall was 14 miles around. Who was this leader? (see page 19)

2. The Battle of Poltava, fought on June 28, 1709, between Russian and Sweden, pitted one great military leader against a ruthless and determined man. Name these two men. (see page 55)

3. At the Battle of Verdun, after absorbing punishing attacks from the German forces, this French general rallied his troops with the these encouraging words, "They shall not pass!" Name this French general and name the two forts that the French lost and later reclaimed. (see page 88).

4. On two separate occasions Kublai Khan amassed a large army and fleet to attack Japan. Khan's forces advanced until typhoons struck - both times - severely crippling the fleets. Since then the Japanese have referred to a "Kamikaze" as something in their favor. What does Kamikaze mean? (see page 35)

5. Instead of capturing New York City, American general George Washington and French general Jean Baptiste de Rochambeau marched their troops into Virginia where they boxed in this British general. Name the British general and the tobacco village where he was cornered. (see page 67)

6. Suleiman the Magnificent was determined to rid the Christians from the heart of the Mediterranean and sent troops to the island of Malta where his troops met the defenses of the Knights of Saint John of Jerusalem at two massive fortresses. Name the two fortresses and identify the one the Turks were unable to defeat. (see page 48)

7. The Battle of Marathon , was an important victory for the Greeks over the Persians. Name the Greek runner who ran the 26 miles to Athens with news of the Greek victory and name the king of the Persians. (see page 9)

8. Name the key city of Battle of the Bulge and the American General who, when demanded by the Germans to surrender, replied with one word, "Nuts." (see page 99)

9. At the Battle of Gettysburg, General Robert E. Lee, over the objections of others, ordered a frontal assault on the Union lines at Cemetery Ridge, resulting in the deaths of many of his troop. Name the Confederate general who led the attack. (see page 78)

10. Name the key battle of the Spanish-American War and the American Lieutenant Colonel who led his men in a valiant charge - seizing victory and fame. (see page 82)

11. Duke William of Normandy contested the crowning of King Harold of England and amassed an army to invade England. The

two armies met on October 14, 1066. Name the battle and identify the victorious army. Duke William of Normandy was also known as two other names. What were they? (see page 29)

12. The turning point of the Battle of Midway came, in a 5 minute window of opportunity, when the U.S. launched 54 of these against the Japanese aircraft carriers. What did the U.S. launch? (see page 94)

13. This Spaniard conquered the Aztec empire in Mexico and in the process defeated the Aztecs on two separate occasions in this city (present-day Mexico City). Name this Spanish conqueror and the city which he twice won. (see page 43)

14. At the Battle of Waterloo, Napoleon hesitated to commit his reserve troops to battle against the British troops of the Duke of Wellington. Had he done so, he probably would have won the day. Why did Napoleon hesitate? (see page 73)

15. During the Second Punic War, the Carthaginians sent this man to lead his men from Spain into Italy, where he met and defeated the Roman army at the Battle of Cannae using this tactical maneuver that trapped the Romans. Name the Carthaginian leader and the maneuver. (see page 15)

16. In 33 BC these two men, fighting for the leadership of Rome, met at sea at the Battle of Actium. Name these two leaders and the woman with whom one was associated. (see page 21)

17. Near the end of WWII which army deployed 2,500,000 men to encircle and conquer the city of Berlin? Name the two generals that commanded that army. (see page 101)

18. The Scottish leader and patriot, Robert the Bruce, challenged the English on the field of Bannockburn in 1314. He divided his men into four schiltrons of pikemen, resembling a Macedonian phalanx. Name the Scottish leader who had developed the formation years earlier. (see page 36)

19. The naval Battle of Trafalgar matched the British fleet against a combined Spanish and French fleet led by the French admiral, Pierre de Villeneuve. Name the British admiral who devised the successful battle plan only to be killed on the deck of his flagship, Victory. (see page 70)

SUGGESTED PROJECTS

1. Many of the battles discussed in this book describe both strategies and tactics used by the opposing forces. Describe the difference between a strategy and a tactic. Find three examples of each in the book.

2. Military leaders often try to find the strengths and weakness of an opponent in order to gain an advanatge. Choose a partner. Each partner chooses a different country. Each partner then makes a list of the others strengths and weaknesses and chooses one weakness to attack. Compare lists and discuss the possible outcome.

INDEX